The
WELLNESS
8

By

Jeremy Reynolds

By
Jeremy Reynolds

directSMARTS
Publishing

Published by directSMARTS Publishing

directSMARTS Publishing
331 S Rio Grande St
Suite 304

Salt Lake City, Utah 84101
801-322-1199
www.directsmarts.com

To order additional copies call 801-322-1199 or
go to www.directsmarts.com or go to www.thewellness8.com

Interior design: deluxemedia
Cover design: TJ Erny, www.rumoradvertising.com

ISBN 13: 978-0692943328
ISBN 10: 0692943323

Printed in the United States of America

CONTENTS

FOREWORD

By Stephen R. Covey

To begin with the end in mind means to start with a clear understanding of your destination. Take the story of Jeremy Reynolds. Jeremy has achieved incredible success time and again by focusing on Habit 2. He started his career in business earning less than $7.00 an hour answering telephones for a nutritional products company. He had the lowest paying job in the company. His position wasn't even on any corporate organizational chart. At that time he set a goal to earn a six-figure salary in that company within six years. He saw a clear vision of himself as the top sales person in the company, and he kept this image in his mind everyday. Six years later Jeremy was with that same nutritional products company, but now he was vice president of international sales. He had reached his goal and was traveling all over the world to meet with customers.

After similar roles of the few other companies Jeremy started his own powder manufacturing company. At the very beginning of this process, he wrote down his goal. Writing is a cycle neuro-muscular activity. It bridges the conscious and the subconscious mind. It literally imprints the subconscious mind. This is the goal he wrote down. To create a powder manufacturing company with $10 million in annual revenues and to be completely debt free. Within three years, Jeremy's little company was on its way to $10 million in annual revenues and he was completely out of debt, mortgage and all.

One day some of Jeremy's customers approached him with a new product they were about to launch. The nature of the product caught Jeremy's attention immediately, and his customers explained that they were leaning towards selling their new product through network marketing. In fact, they asked Jeremy about his interest in becoming a founding distributor to take the product to market. Jeremy was shocked by the offer. He wasn't sure if he was the right person, but he agreed to come on as the founding distributor under one condition. Not having a network marketing background, Jeremy told them that he would come on board if he could prove to himself that he could make it work. They all agreed on a goal of $250,000 in product sales in 60 days. Again starting from nothing but a goal in mind, Jeremy invited ten people to his home to listen to the story of this new product. He didn't even have any product samples or fancy presentations to show that first night. The next day his family room was packed with 25 more people interested in learning about the product and business opportunity.

Jeremy missed his target of $250,000 in 60 days. He actually sold $1,750,000. What has happened in the three years since has exceeded anything he imagined at the time. Jeremy and his wife Karen reached multi millionaire status.

He works out of his home office and he now has time that he never had before to spend with his family. Jeremy has mastered Habit 2 and he begins each endeavor with the end in mind. He has the ability to imagine himself having, being or doing something in the future and he sees that image so clearly that it becomes completely real to him as he moves closer toward it everyday. Intellectual creation always precedes physical creation. How different our lives are when we really know what is deeply important to us and we manage ourselves each day to be and do what matters most.[i]

From the book, *The Seven Habits of Successful Network Marketing Professionals*, published by FranklinCovey.

ACKNOWLEDGMENTS

This book is really the synergistic product of a team of people. Without their passionate and unique contributions it would have never been written. Each of their names could easily be listed on the cover alongside mine, and I express my deep appreciation to them.

- My incredible wife, Karen, for many of the ideas and reminders of the stories in the book, for her constant support and encouragement, for her intuitive wisdom and her education in wellness and fitness, and above all, her sacrifice and dedication for more than two decades as my best friend and business partner on the home-front, raising our three children in wellness.

- My dear children, McKinley, her husband Tad Carter, McKayla, and PJ, and their spouses and children to come, for their patience, love and kindness and for their lives and contributions.

- Craig Case, for his superb management of this whole production process, his positive energy, his remarkable judgment, and counseling on major key issues, and his work hand in glove with our editor, producer, and training teams.

- Breck England, for his incredible ability to take an idea and concept and give it life through words. His editorial ability in weaving the ideas, stories, transcripts, and research together in an amazing way is unmatched.

- Porter Hall, Stephen Hall, Jeff Graham, Shane O'Toole, Tyler Sohm, Ryo Sambongi, Toshi Kurogi, and Mark & Alma Carter for their willingness to go above and Beyond in every respect!

-To the Brooks family, who laid the foundation for us to build on for the last decade, and where I have learned many valuable lessons. And to our extended family in health and wealth around the globe who have found The Wellness 8 in the most unique and powerful ways. Our most loyal partners Butch & Carolyn Swaby, Sherm & Ruth Smith, Dana & Mike Alsop, Connie Hollstein, Dr. Dan & Esther Sollee, Joe & Kathy Duncan, John McDermott, Doreen Carter, Felix & Lisa Gudino, Don & Susie Smart, and Gale Wong, and the rest...you know who you are. I love you all.

-To my core wellness 8 team of professional advisors past & present: David Parkinson, Ladd Johnson, Mike Minnoch, Peter Sommer, David Wenk, Eric Jackson, Bud Heaton and Jason Muir.

- My brothers, Jeff Reynolds, his wife Candice, Spencer Reynolds, his wife Tricia and to my sisters, Kim Kohlhase, her husband Randy, and M'Lisa Frandsen and her husband Eric, and their children that round out the Reynolds' family. Each of you has had a profound influence in my life and I am forever grateful.

- My dear Mother, Janiell Reynolds Vashon for her lifelong love, loyalty and friendship, her living example of living The Wellness 8 daily, and her amazing example of building networks dedicated to wellness and friendships all around the globe. Also, to her husband Adrian for his love and support.

- And finally to my father, friend and now spiritual mentor, Paul Reynolds. I love you dad and I'm grateful for your guiding light in my journey.

TURNING POINT

I vividly remember a conversation I had many years ago, which marked a turning point in my leadership journey. I was sitting at a Holiday Inn with a friend, when he asked me if I had a personal growth plan. I didn't.
In fact, I didn't even know you were supposed to have one.

- John C. Maxwell

There have been many turning points in my life.

At age 19, I developed Crohn's colitis, an inflammatory bowel disease that affects the lining of the digestive tract and, if not closely managed, can cause havoc. It came just as I was getting ready to go to Eastern Europe to serve as a missionary for my church. This disease turned my life into all sort of unpredictable directions.

When I was 32, my wife Karen and I made the decision to purchase a struggling manufacturing plant that was losing money. That was a big, risky turning point for us. A few years later, after we had the good fortune of turning the business around, we sold the company and became master distributors of a new direct selling business. Now that was really a ride!

But the one point on which my life turned most profoundly was my dad's passing in 1996. He died of prostate cancer, a common disease that many men must deal with. My dad was a great person, a great husband, and a fine father. He and my mom raised my brothers and sisters in an upper-middle-class home in a fine community where we were loved and our needs were met.

We knew for several months that his death was coming, but it shook me up just the same. He was diagnosed with his disease at 48 and died eighteen months later. I was 23 at the time, and I realized with a shock that if I died at the same age as my dad, I was already almost half way through. It gave me a sense of urgency in ways nothing had before. At his funeral I decided to make the best of things and to get going with my life.

I learned a lot from my dad, especially in the last few months of his life as he spent time with each of his kids, teaching us what he knew and giving us advice on how to live more effectively. Throughout this book, I will share with you some of the things he taught me that I value so much now.

When I bought the struggling nutritional-supplement manufacturing company, I decided that I was going to make the most of it and turn it around. I chose to run the business using the principles my dad taught me and to get the most out of every day. It was a hectic time, but, with hard work and the blessings of God, I succeeded. The attitude that every day matters, became a big part of my life when my dad died. There was an underlying urgency that kept me focused and on track.

When problems arose and things got in the way (as they always do), I said to myself, "I don't have time to dwell on negatives. I'm on a mission here. I need to do this for my family. I am stronger than this requires." And I was. I was set on accomplishing all the things that I wanted in life by the time I got to be my dad's age—and now that's only a few years away. I hope to live another 50 years beyond that! But if I don't, I will have made my mark and done the best I could.

In this book you'll discover what I've discovered. We'll drill down into each one of eight dimensions of total "wellness." I call them the "Wellness 8." Wellness is more than just an absence of physical ailments. We can be physically healthy and still not be "well." If we are emotionally, socially, or spiritually sick, we are not "well."

When people ask me how I'm doing, I want to be able to say, "I'm well!"— and mean it in every way. I want to be emotionally, financially, intellectually, socially, and spiritually well, in addition to being physically well—and so do you.

In the next chapter we'll describe each of the Wellness 8, then how each generation can apply the Wellness 8, and in the rest of the book we'll explore how you can grow personally beyond anything you've imagined if you'll make the Wellness 8 a focus in your life.

I don't set myself up as an example, but I have learned without any doubt that living by these 8 principles is essential to a well-lived life. My dad knew this secret, and although he died too young, his was a well-lived life. And my dad set the stage for my life.

Thanks for that, Dad.

THE WELLNESS 8

From my own research and from my dad's precious teaching I've extracted eight basic dimensions of wellness: emotional, environmental, financial, intellectual, occupational, physical, social, and spiritual. I can almost hear my dad's voice teaching me correct principles in each of these dimensions. In many ways, he personified every one of the dimensions:

Emotional
My dad was kind and consistently thoughtful. He had it right inside.

Environmental
Make your surroundings the best you can. Surround yourself with the best people you can. He was the best at that.

Financial
I learned from him the principles of debt-free and prosperous living. He gave it his best but kept coming up short , but he worked with me and inspired me to get it right.

Intellectual
I learned so much of what I know about thinking and studying from my dad. Never stop learning or you start dying.

Occupational

I worked closely with him for six years and saw how he ran a successful business: with integrity, hard work, and dedication.

 ## Physical.

My dad inspired me to stay in shape, and we actually worked together for a health-and-fitness company.

 ## Social.

Nobody was friendlier than my dad. Ask anybody who knew my dad—they will tell you that everybody loved him. He always smiled, always was the one that you wanted to be around.

Spiritual.

I learned about God and about love from my dad. But most importantly I learned the importance of just being a good person. For that I am so grateful.

This book is about what I am learning. It's about eight things to do to get life right. It's like a wheel with eight spokes. If just one of the spokes is broken or missing, the whole ride is bumpy at best—and ruined at worst.

I call them the Wellness 8. In life, wellness is more than just being healthy. It's about doing well and even more about being well. I could be physically toned and have lots of money and be the life of the party and still have a miserable life. Each of the Wellness 8 is about the kind of person I am, not just the stuff I do or the things I have.

We begin down inside the human heart with Emotional Wellness. I believe that healthy living begins with the emotions. People who are sharing, contributing and making a difference are emotionally well.

People in emotional turmoil can't get their lives right in any other dimension, but once they are at peace inside, they can move forward with greater ease.

The environmental dimension is all about managing your personal surroundings to bypass the negative (people, thoughts, media, self-talk) and to increase the positive (serving and sharing with others). It necessarily follows emotional wellness. My emotional life is like a well of water. If it stagnates, I'll be a source of poison to the outside world. If I do the things that create good emotional health, like reading good books, exercising, meditating, doing regular deep breathing exercises, the water springs, flows, expands, and becomes fresh and overflows the well. As it overflows, the water nourishes the environment: helping and healing others and contributing to their lives.

A person who is emotionally well (on the inside) and environmentally well (on the outside) is set up to be financially well. Financial wellness is not only about money; in my opinion, it's about the richness you feel when you're making a meaningful difference in other people's lives. That richness is true financial and business success. It's the unbelievable feeling of gratitude and caring that only comes when you are in the service of others.

Intellectual and occupational wellness are about doing creative, stimulating work and learning all you can. Two sides of one coin, your mind and your life's work need constant renewal or both will stagnate. "Reading for fun" can actually give you new ideas that will change your approach to business. And if you're constantly aware, you can learn tremendous life lessons from your work. Your occupation can feed your mind, and vice versa; in fact, if it's not happening, both your customers and your brain will go numb on you.

Physical wellness is about maintaining a quality of life so you can keep contributing, growing, and learning. It's about exercise, yes, but maybe even more it's about your diet and the good feeling you get from "being well."

Social wellness is not so much about having a good time as giving a good time to others. It's about doing something nice for somebody else just for the joy of it. Occasionally, when in the drive-through at a fast-food restaurant, I'll pay for the order of the person behind me in line. They aren't expecting it. They're like, "What? Who is that? Oh my gosh!" Twice they've actually pulled up and said, "Thank-you so much! That was so kind. Do I know you?" I was like, "No. But now go and do something nice for somebody else." It was so fun. Social wellness is about being kind just for the heck of it. It's amazing how it makes you feel.

Spiritual wellness is the highest form of wellness. It's about inner peace and joy. It's about meaning and purpose. Without spiritual wellness, you will always be dissatisfied, deep-down hungry for something that matters beyond just indulging yourself.

We recently approached the local YWCA and asked them how we could help the disadvantaged population they serve. They were like, "Are you kidding? We have 130 kids who come from challenging families with huge needs. Our big goal right now is to give each of these kids a backpack with school supplies." I said, "Done." We found a sponsor for each kid and had a great event with the kids and their families. In each backpack was a letter of encouragement from the sponsor. We held an outdoor movie and a big barbecue. Every kid felt special and great, and so did their sponsors. That's the kind of thing people do to gain spiritual wellness.

That's what this book is about: total wellness. It's about moving the inward (emotional wellness) to the outward (social wellness) and back again to the most inward part of you—spiritual wellness.

When we speak of total wellness, we're not talking about big, life-changing steps. Because, believe it or not, it's the little steps you take that end up being the most transformative of all. So far in my life I've discovered that if I do just a few things each day to take care of the Wellness 8, everything eventually works out . . . well, really well!

One more thing: How you live by the Wellness 8 depends a lot on how old you are.

Things that work for Baby Boomers don't necessarily work for Millennials, and Generation Xers look at life in unique ways, so each generation will use the Wellness 8 in unique ways. In this book we'll explore how your concerns differ from the concerns of other generations. At the end of each chapter we'll see how you might choose to apply the Wellness 8 depending on your generation. Then, at the end of the book, you can find an addendum that explains all about the number of differences among the generations in greater detail.

Now let's get into the Wellness 8!

EMOTIONAL WELLNESS

Our attitude toward life determines life's attitude towards us.

- Earl Nightingale

Our exploration of the eight dimensions begins with the emotional dimension.

Why?

Because everything begins with how we think—particularly with how we think about ourselves. In the book *Mindset,* Stanford psychologist Carol S. Dweck, Ph.D., teaches that your success in life depends almost completely on how you think about yourself and your talents and abilities.

Dweck explains that people tend to have one of two mindsets. People with a fixed mindset—those who believe that abilities and talents are rigidly fixed—are less likely to succeed in most everything. On the other hand, people with a growth mindset—those who believe that abilities can be learned, developed, and leveraged—are more success-ful across every area of life. [ii]

Emotionally well people have a mindset of growth, possibility, and positivity. Strangely enough, emotional wellness has a lot less to do with your feelings than with your thinking. That may not sound right, but it is. If you believe you can grow, change, improve, and enjoy the process, you will have emotional wellness and you will, in turn, be far more likely to succeed in life.

Where does your mindset come from? Clearly there's no single answer. Your mindset comes from countless positive and negative experiences with your parents, teachers, and friends. It comes from your attempts to use your talents and abilities. The good news, says Dweck, is that your mindset—your mental picture of yourself and your possibili-ties—is pliable: at any time, anyone can learn how to develop a growth mindset to achieve greater success and happiness.

Your belief in your ability to change things about yourself and your en-vironment is where self-improvement and happiness begin. All of the other wellness dimensions start here because without this emotional wellness, you won't find wellness elsewhere.

So how do you develop a growth mindset? How do you become "emo-tionally well"?

Your mindset starts with that mental dialogue that plays over and over in your mind throughout the day. It's found in how we talk to our-selves. So becoming aware of your self-talk is the first step to emotional wellness.

So much of what we tell ourselves is just not true. Some experts suggest that up to 70%[iii] of self-talk is negative. Do any of these internal sound bites look familiar?

- **"Why am I such a loser?"**
- **"How come I'm always late?"**
- **"I just can't lose weight?"**
- **"No one likes me."**

We remember all the negative things our parents, siblings, friends, or teachers said to us. We remember the negative reactions from others that diminished how we felt about ourselves. Throughout the years, we've played these messages over and over so many times that they've become part of our mindset about ourselves. They fuel our feelings of anger, fear, guilt, and hopelessness. The negatives influence our failure or success, and ultimately, our happiness and our sorrows.

Negative thinking is very habit-forming. It comes from years of poor self-talk – from the lies we tell ourselves about ourselves, and from negative people we interact with. There are a lot of negative people in the world, and they make a lot of racket. They're like Chicken Little, the fabled character who decided that the world was coming to an end when an acorn landed on his head. He ran around yelling, *"The sky is falling! We're all gonna die!"*

Of course, nothing was further from the truth. Jim Rohn famously said, *"We are the average of the five people we spend the most time with."* [iv] So get the negative people out of your life. Hang with people who are genuinely upbeat, positive, and happy!

Negative thinking also comes from our environment—from what we are exposed to. The world is a frightening place. The news is scary—so much so that I've stopped watching the news on TV and I don't listen to it when I'm traveling. Instead, I listen to good books and to upbeat, inspiring podcasts. The news always made me feel negative because it dwells on the negative.

In fact, I hardly watch TV at all. I'm not claiming everybody should give up TV—not at all. For us, however, we have no TV service in any of our homes, and we haven't for years. There are just too many other good things to be doing besides watching people shooting each other.

Here's a funny story. A few years ago our church was having a Fathers' Day program and they polled all the kids and asked, *"What is your dad's favorite TV show?"* My son PJ was four years old at the time. They put their responses in a cute little insert that they passed out to everyone in the congregation. Some of the answers were football or the different TV programs that were on TV at the time. PJ's answer was, *"My dad doesn't watch TV. He's productive."* Imagine that from a four-year-old!

My point is, check your negative self-talk and the people you choose to be with, and do some proactive things to improve the quality of your internal dialogue and your relationships. One of the ways to recognize optimism, hope, and joy is to intentionally fill your thoughts with positive self-talk. Positive self-talk actually rewires in your brain. Good things start happening when you do this. Look for positives and stay away from negatives. It will have a dramatic impact on your mindset and which emotions you experience.

If there are things that are getting you down, avoid them. Stop listening to negativity. Stop listening to the music that might be wearing you down instead of lifting you up. Start finding more positive influences than negative influences. Start looking for light rather than dark. Find ways to be uplifted and get it right inside so you're at peace within yourself. We all need to proactively put more positives into our life.

When I was on a recent flight, as the plane was taxiing, the flight attendant demonstrated how to put on an oxygen mask. She made the point that the adults should put their masks on first before helping children or others who need it. In other words, "Take care of yourself first. You won't be much help to anyone else if you don't have the oxygen you need." Well said. If we get the emotional dimension right, we're in a much better place to be of service to others.

I use a couple of tools to help me manage my emotions. First, daily meditation, and second, deep breathing exercises. These tools help me deal with the stressors and challenges in my own life and allow me to be the best version of myself for the people around me. It's wonderful to be able to look inside myself and say, *I know how to calm my own mind so that I don't get worked up in stressful times."*

Most of us have much to cope with. Many of us go from one crisis to the next without taking any time to be quiet, to reflect, to consider, to be inspired. The pressure is always on. We manage crises all day, and when the day is done we are mentally exhausted. And often we've been marginally productive.

I've learned that in order to be emotionally healthy, I have to take a mental break, to let my brain relax every few hours. Regardless of how busy I am, it's important to take ten or fifteen minutes, put down my cell phone, and walk around the block or do some deep breathing exercises and enjoy a quiet moment. Significant research supports the idea of finding a quiet place three or four times during the workday away from technology and screens to meditate, to get quiet, and to breathe consciously. Some people call this meditation.

Quiet, deep breathing is a great stress reliever. Right now, while you're reading this book, take a deep breath and hold it. Push out your stomach and let the air into your lungs. Feel the wave of nitrogen, oxygen and carbon dioxide press against the bounds of your ribcage and swell your lungs. Hold it. . . . Now exhale. Repeat.

Conscious, controlled breathing provides a clear path into your subconscious mind. This is part of the logic behind Lamaze techniques, and the breathing practiced in meditation, yoga, and even in everyday wisdom. Have you ever told someone who is freaking out to slow down and to "take a deep breath"? When they do that, they can think again. Controlled breathing promises a kind of visceral self-knowledge, a more perfect melding of mind and body that regulates your emotions.

Lynn Goldberg, my friend and meditation coach is co-founder of a cool app called Breethe. She taught me an exercise called Balance Breath. Try it with me right now. Sit with your back straight while you're learning the exercise. First, exhale completely through your mouth.. Close your mouth and inhale quietly through your nose and mentally count to four. Count slowly. One, two, three, four. Next, hold your breath and mentally count to four. One, two, three, four. Now, exhale completely through your mouth, to a count of four. One, two, three, four. Then repeat!

Okay! How do you feel? Noticeably less stressed? It always works. That simple technique will help you to find a better emotional state. Use it whenever you feel a little stressed.

I have learned that I can use this technique to relax my mind in virtually any situation. Afterwards I feel much better and I can think more clearly.

I love what Viktor Frankl says, *"Between stimulus and response there is a space. In that space is our power to choose our response. In our response lies our growth and our freedom."* ᵛ I can react to stress, or when I'm going to act foolishly, I can step back and do a balance breath deep breathing exercise. It helps me to be proactive rather than reactive. If somebody yells at me or comes at me and is viciously attacking me, or whatever it may be, I don't need to respond with a punch or a throw or a reaction that's negative. I can actually assess the situation, take a breath, and think through in my mind a simple series of responses: "How am I going to react? What's the best reaction?" If you develop the deep-breathing habit, you can do it in a split second, and it can make all of the difference to your emotional well-being.

I use the Breethe app every day as a guide for meditation and mindfulness. I love it because it works on both the conscious and subconscious mind. It works even when I maybe doze off during the session. It is incredibly helpful.

We have to get past the idea of having a "bad day." "I stubbed my toe this morning. Now that's going to set off my emotions for the rest of the day." Remember, how we act and how we feel is ultimately a choice. It's up to us to proactively become what it is that we want to be.

It doesn't matter who's slamming you. It doesn't matter that you stubbed your toe, or the business meeting went badly, or who cut you off in traffic, or that sales prospect wasn't interested. It doesn't matter what just happened. You can get down, angry, frustrated, fearful, decide you're done for—or you can make someone's life happier.

So emotional stability comes from awareness that you do have some control over how you think and how you feel. It comes from paying attention to your self-talk, proactively eliminating negatives in your life, hanging with positive people, taking time to be quiet, and making conscious breathing exercises a habit.

APPLICATION

Boomers and Emotional Wellness

Good news for Boomers: In general, people become more emotionally mature and stable as they age. They're slower to anger and more likely to forgive.

If you're a Boomer, you can take advantage of your more mellow emotions to offset some of the radical changes you're facing. As your career and your children fade into the background of your life, you could become depressed. It's normal to feel that way when the things that were so much a part of your life get disrupted. But again, pay attention to your self-talk. If you're calling yourself "over the hill" or a "has-been" or a "failure," decide to stop it and start relying on your accumulated wisdom.

Let go of those destructive patterns of thought. They take up too much energy. Instead learn to calm your mind with the breathing and other mindfulness exercises described in this chapter.

Gen Xers and Emotional Wellness

Gen Xers are probably the most stressed-out generation. The difficult economics of life today, along with a somewhat cynical mindset, make Gen Xers emotionally strained and tense.

If you're a Gen Xer you can find a great deal of relief from meditation as described in this chapter. The good news is that meditation, yoga, and other mindfulness techniques are popular with Gen Xers, so you won't be alone in making the effort.

Millennials and Emotional Wellness

Millennials are a stressed-out group. Relationship problems, the difficulty and expense of getting an education, the competition for jobs, and the high expectation of finding just the right job—these factors combine to make your life pretty tense if you're a Millennial.

According to psychological studies, Millennials tend to cope with stress by drinking too much, hanging out and playing games too much, or spending too much money. A better way to achieve emotional wellness is to practice the meditation and breathing exercises described in this chapter. It's also a lot less expensive! Get the Breethe app and let Lynne be your meditation coach too, you'll thank me later.

ENVIRONMENTAL WELLNESS

Change your thoughts and you change your world.

– Norman Vincent Peale

A good friend of mine has a son who struggles with drug addiction. After years of dealing with the ramifications of drug abuse, his son finally wanted to stop using, so he entered and successfully completed a rehab program. But a few months later, he relapsed. My friend learned that overcoming drugs is a process, not an event, and that most users relapse, multiple times. He learned that in order to stay sober, his son needed to make three changes. He needed to change his playground, his playmates and his play toys. In other words, he needed to change his environment.

Webster's definition of an environment is the "surroundings or conditions in which a person, animal, or plant lives and operates." In order to permanently stay off drugs, my friend's son needed to change his personal environment: Only then was he able to change who he was and who he could become.

So how do you go about changing your environment to be more effective, healthier, and happier?

First, you have to decide what in your environment is holding you back. Is it clutter, unprofitable relationships, bad habits, undone projects, time-wasters, negative vibes from your music, even the lighting in your room? You have to know where to start and what you need to change.

A good first step to improving your environment is clearing out the clutter from your physical space. I'm talking about your stuff! Choose a day and clean out a room that is bugging you. Take the clothes that you don't wear anymore to the thrift store. Get rid of the old stuff that isn't used, even if it's still good, and let someone else use it. Get rid of the piles of stuff cluttering up your space. You'll be astonished at how much better it feels. It's like shedding 30 pounds of unwanted weight from your body. Do it in one room and then do it in another. Clean out your closets and your garage.

If for whatever reason, if you can't do it by yourself, ask someone to help. Depending on the company and where you live, professional organizers charge between $30 and $80 per hour to help you organize and throw stuff away. You will be astonished at the stuff you have lying around that you no longer need or want but that you haven't used in years. Do it.

Now, I'm not just talking about the physical clutter, but your emotional clutter as well. Some of us are stuck, unable to progress because of the clutter in our minds. Emotional clutter holds us back, keeps us spinning our wheels. Think about your unkept commitments, the incomplete projects and goals you've let slide, and all of the painful mental noise going on in your brain. How about the people who are negative toward you, the people you've let down or disappointed, the people you need to forgive, or those you want forgiveness from? Whatever it may be, all of those things are negatively effecting your personal environment.

How many of us have negative relationships that are killing us—keeping us from progressing and growing?

Now my friend and his son regularly go to twelve-step program meetings. He says that it's one of the most important things he's ever experienced. The program has taught him how to let go of past offenses and unmet expectations, of disappointments, and of people he has been angry with. He has learned how to forgive and how to seek forgiveness.

This idea of letting go of the past is profound. It is a key to addiction recovery and is a foundational principle for emotional and spiritual growth. I love what bestselling author Steve Maraboli says, *"Letting go means to come to the realization that some people are a part of your history, but not a part of your destiny."* Regardless of what has happened in our lives, we don't have to be tied to the past. We can improve our environment simply by letting go.

Where do you spend most of your time? Some people are more beautiful, talented, or rich than others, but time is the great leveler. Everybody gets exactly the same amount of time every day. Using time well makes all of the difference. It's amazing how much time many people waste everyday doing things that not only don't help, but also do damage.

I maintain that TV is a big time waster. Most American children spend about three hours a day watching TV. Added together, all types of screen time total between five to seven hours a day.[vi] Now, there are only so many hours in a day. If a kid spends six hours a day watching a screen, that is six hours he or she could be doing other things, like reading *Treasure Island,* shooting baskets, playing kick the can, (remember kick the can?) or just staring up at the clouds (an enormously healthy thing to do!).

As people get older, screen time increases. Teen-agers spend nine hours in front of screens.[vii] According to a 2014 Nielsen report, the average American adult over the age of 18 spends almost 12 hours per day on electronic gadgets.[viii] Admittedly, much of that time is work related. Still, according to the New York Times, on average, American adults are watching five hours and four minutes of television per day, every day.[ix]

Wow! Think about it. What could you be doing with your brain during that time? Pay attention to how you use your time every day. If you track it for a week or two, you will be surprised. It will change how you use your time—which could be a really good thing.

For all its benefits, social media can be a big time waster, and it can set up all sorts of false expectations to inhibit our progress. Paradoxically, while many people have dozens of social-media friends, their influence with those friends is shrinking. You would think that we would be reaching out to others, but social media is having the opposite effect. People are in cocoons, texting on their phones, looking at Instagram, thinking they're having these great socially rich experiences, when in fact their personal environment is pretty bland.

Studies now show how Instagram and other social media sites negatively affect self-esteem and promote self-loathing.[x] How about these tidbits?

"Instagram, Instagram, tell me who I really am."

"Facebook, Facebook, tell me how my life should look."

Because of the photo-shopped, unrealistic images and lifestyles presented on these sites, the social bar is set way too high. We are comparing ourselves against those who have spent hours on a post, perfecting a millisecond in time. When you look at a picture of a family standing on a beach, and everyone's attractive, pristine and amazing, wearing classy clothes, and they're all positioned perfectly, we get this idea that that's the way it is all of the time.

But any one of us who has ever been there knows that the picture is nothing other than a split second in time. That perfect existence is what we want to portray to the Facebook world, when in fact, nothing could be further from the truth. In reality, the second after the shutter goes off, a wave crashes up on the beach and soaks everybody. The little kids run off in five different directions, and the mom screams at the dad. Dad is thinking there isn't enough money in the account to pay for the vacation and the new clothes that everyone is wearing, let alone to pay the photographer.

None of this gets communicated in the perfect Facebook picture. Reality is what happens before and after the shutter goes off. But we constantly compare ourselves to a false idea of other peoples' perfect lives. What a tragedy.

Don't try to live up to someone else's social media posts. Nothing good ever comes from making comparisons. Either you feel superior, which is just plain not true, or you feel inferior, which is also an outright lie. Be authentic in what you do and in who you are. You'll experience greater peace in your personal environment if you do.

Who you spend time with is a big part of your personal environment. The idea that you're the sum total of the five people you hang with is absolutely true. We do gradually become like the people around us. Are the people you hang with negative or positive? Do they lift you up, or bring you down? If you want a socio-economic lift, hang out with people who make more money than you do. If you want a spiritual lift, hang around with people who are kinder, more caring, and more spiritual than you are. You'll become more like them. It is a natural law.

Is your personal environment filled with worry? Five hundred years ago, the French philosopher Michel de Montaigne said: *"My life has been filled with terrible misfortune; most of which never happened."* It's amazing how worry wreaks havoc on your environment.

A recent study looked into how many of our worries ever materialize. Subjects were asked to write down their past worries and then identify which of their imagined misfortunes never actually happened. It turns out that 85 percent of what subjects worried about never came to pass; and with the 15 percent that did happen, 79 percent of subjects discovered either they could handle the problem better than expected, or they learned a worthwhile lesson from the problem. This means that 97 percent of what you worry over is not much more than a fearful mind punishing you with exaggerations and misperceptions.

Once Karen and I took our family to the redwoods of Northern California. The trees there are enormous—the biggest living things on the planet. While we were there I learned that redwood trees need plenty of space to grow. They need an open forest and plenty of the right nutrition. They need the right environment to reach their potential. If they get it, they grow and grow and grow.

At the gift shop in the park they sell redwood seedlings in small containers. These seedlings are the very beginnings of the 300-foot-tall mammoths. The idea is you could take one of these redwood seedlings home, plant it, and someday, theoretically, long after you and your family have expired, there could be a huge redwood tree growing in the front yard.

The reality is this won't happen, as most of the little tiny trees die because they will be placed in an environment that constrains, rather than supports what redwood trees need to grow. They need to be able to spread out and spread their root systems to aquifers to be able to create those majestic trees. Some people keep them in the small buckets that they were in when they bought them. But the trees stay small because of the constraint of the bucket. They can't grow and reach their potential.

As I was pondering these giants, it dawned on me that people are kind of like redwood trees. I asked my family, *"Hey, how big is your bucket?"* They looked at me puzzled. I explained my thinking and one by one, they got what I was talking about. Then I asked, *"Are you a mature redwood giant, or are you still a little seedling in the bucket? Is your environment supporting or inhibiting your growth?"*

And I ask you the same question. What's holding you back from reaching your potential, from becoming a mature redwood tree rather than a stumpy seedling?

APPLICATION

Baby Boomers and Environmental Wellness

Boomers worry a lot about quality of life as they age. "What will happen to me as I get older and less capable?" The good news for Boomers is that they are at the height of their wisdom and experience. They are also in relatively good health and will probably live longer than any other generation in history.

A lack of money or a sense of purpose dooms many retirees to a life watching television at home, which simply leads to more depression and discouragement. What a tragedy if they waste the last 30 years of an otherwise productive life sitting in front of a TV screen. Boomers need to surround themselves with "a bigger bucket" to grow in—full of the things that nourish social, intellectual, and spiritual wellness. You'll find those things in this book. Decide today to do something, learn something, or try something new.

Gen Xers and Environmental Wellness

Generation X is called "the Worried Generation." Many have big concerns over job and family stability and future retirement. They are caught up in what's known as the "midlife crisis." They are also known as the "Squeezed Generation," squeezed for time and money, squeezed between caring for aging parents and dependent children.

The good news is that Gen Xers are smarter, better educated, and healthier than their parents' generation. It's hard to avoid worrying, but if you're a Gen Xer, try putting aside most of your worries—they will never materialize anyway. Focus on creating a positive environment for yourself. You're a redwood: you need space in your life to grow. Enjoy watching your children grow instead of constantly worrying about them. Give them space to grow. A quick exercise to stop the worry is to write down the three things you are most grateful for. Get your mind off your worries by counting your blessings today.

Millennials and Environmental Wellness

Millennials have to be really careful with the time they spend on social media, which is a big part of their environment. They spend even more time than the other generations watching the big screen—but not cable TV shows. They spend four times the number of hours on game consoles and digital streaming than their older counterparts. This is the "Gaming Generation."

Three out of four Millennials spend more than two hours a day on their phones, but not talking. Social media stars are their celebrities. All in all, Millennials can spend as much as 18 hours a day skimming social media, working digitally, watching TV, texting, or playing games.

With all the excitement and learning possibilities on the media, Millennials so fixed to their screens obviously need more variety in their environment. If you're a Millennial, think about the environment you're creating for yourself. Is it totally focused on screens? Do you take time to walk and breathe in a park? Do you visit with your family members? Do you go to lunch with a friend? Pick one and make it a priority today. When you do, put away the screens while you do. Enjoy the present.

Is your "bucket" so small—so focused on a screen—that you can't grow as a person and become totally "well"?

FINANCIAL WELLNESS

If you will live like no one else, later, you can live like no one else.

– Dave Ramsey

T his chapter is about money and things.

A person's attitude toward money and possessions determines to a great degree their wellness and their happiness.

Ben Franklin penned the insight *"Time is Money."* While that may not be quite true, money is related to time. The management of money, like the management of time, affects how much good you can do in the world. (Franklin also is credited with saying, *"He who says that money does not buy happiness does not know how to spend his money!"*)

Given the choice between more time and more money, which would you generally pick? Would you pay more for a direct flight to Hawaii to gain a couple of extra hours on the beach? Would you take a better-paying, high-stress job that requires many late nights at the office and a lot of out-of-town travel?

A friend of mine recently faced such a decision. It wasn't a big deal, but it required that he decide what was most important to him at that moment. He had the chance to make some good money at an out-of-state job over a weekend. But he had a baby girl born a few months earlier and a wife who desperately needed his help at home

Which to choose? The extra pay for his time, or the time with his family?

The answer really comes down to which choice is more important in the long term. With money, we often make short-term decisions that relieve immediate pain or indulge immediate pleasure but don't require discipline. It is easier to make short-term decisions that have tremendous long-term consequences.

Let me share a little bit about what my dad taught me about money. It wasn't from his example. Rather, it was what I learned with him in the twilight of his life that transformed me.

We lived well. My dad drove nice cars and had good jobs. We lived in a nice part of town and went to good schools. True to Boomer form, my mother was a stay-at-home mom. On the outside, everything looked great, but I grew up watching my dad struggle with his ever-present yellow pad, vainly trying to make the numbers work. No matter how much money there was, it was never enough at the end of the month.

At some point, I decided that I didn't want to live like that. I didn't want the pain of never having enough money. It really bugged me, and my dad could see that. He was pretty perceptive and realized this was an issue for me. So, when it became clear that he only had a few months to live, he sat down with me in a candid father-to-son talk and explained that one of the most important things I could get right was money management. And I'd say, "Yeah, dad, I remember those yellow pads. If there is a better way, tell me about it."

And he said, "I found something. Would you be willing to listen to it with me?" What he found was a John Cummuta program on tape—Debt Free and Prosperous Living—all about money management. We would listen to a chapter and then have a little discussion about it. He knew how important it was to me. He saw my motivation, and he knew how I was wired.

When I see a good book about finances, I pick it up and read it cover to cover because of that time spent with my dad.

When Dave Ramsey came along I embraced everything he taught. I listened to his CD's and attended all of his seminars. Dave Ramsey's Financial Peace University is a gem. I shared it with my wife. Ramsey resonated with her, too, and we started using his envelope system just as he described it. Following through on it, we developed strong financial discipline from the envelope system. The envelope system is when you cash your check and actually put the cash in different envelopes, and you pay your bills from those envelopes. The envelopes represent the different categories of your budget. It creates a dramatic visual that allows you to see exactly how much money you have left in a given category by taking a quick peek in your envelope. We did it for a couple of years and it taught us so much. Karen managed it and kept us on track. It created incredible financial understanding and discipline that continues to keep us on track to this day.

For anyone who wants greater control over their personal finances, two books I recommend are Robert Kiyosaki's *Rich Dad Poor Dad*, and *The Cashflow Quadrant*. *Rich Dad Poor Dad* sets the stage for understanding that everyone has power to manage their finances – if they want to. *The Cashflow Quadrant* made me realize that I needed to stop being an employee and start being an independent contractor, even if I was working for somebody else—partially because of the tax advantages. As an employee, I have little control over my taxes because of the withdrawal laws, but as an independent contractor, I can manage my own taxes. *Cashflow Quadrant* is brilliant for learning about the flow of cash and how it can work to your benefit.

In summary, the books on finance that have helped me most are:

- *Debt-Free and Prosperous Living* – John Cummata
- *Financial Peace University* – Dave Ramsey
- *Rich Dad Poor Dad* and *Cashflow Quadrant* - Robert Kiyosaki
- *No Down Payment* - Carlton Sheets
- *Multiple Streams of Income* - Robert Allen

From these books, I have learned that financial wellness is more about financial discipline than about making money. I know too many people who have made a lot of money but who have nothing to show for it because they didn't learn the principles of financial discipline.

From the lessons in these books and my own experience, I recommend five important actions to take for your own financial wellness:

1. Own a business.

If you want to get ahead in life, you cannot be an employee. You will always be working for someone else's dream unless you have your own business. You will always be at the mercy of someone else's dream because you are not in control when you're an employee. Plus, the 40-year career with retirement at the end is no longer the rule. That model's dying. So the idea of adding value to an organization by being an independent contractor is the right way to go for a number of reasons—most importantly for tax reasons.

2. Use the principle of leverage.

If you were to ask Bill Gates when he was running Microsoft what his advantage was, he would have said, *"36,000 employees."* By motivating his employees to put in just one extra hour, he could actually produce 36,000 more hours of effort. That's how he became the richest man in the world. That's the power of leverage.

That's also a big reason why I honestly believe that direct selling is a great way to own a business. In addition to the tax savings that it provides, direct selling offers unbelievable leverage. I can share a product I believe in with other people, who then share it with others, who share it with others. All I've got to do is teach people how to teach other people. And if you can do that, you can leverage your time a hundred to one, or a thousand to one.

Here's the idea: would you rather have 100 percent of your own efforts, or one percent of 100 other people's efforts? I'll take the one percent of 100 people's efforts any day, because if I can motivate 100 people to do 1% more today, I've doubled my capacity. No one's really working any harder, but now I have two times the growth.

And if I can show each person how to do 10% more, some will stay put, others will do 10% more, but some will go from one to 30% more—and all of a sudden I can have a number that's out of all proportion to what I can do myself. I can actually leverage the time of 100 to grow unbelievable wealth beyond all imagination.

I can only work so many hours a week. I can work 40 or 60 or 90 hours a week and kill myself with work—but if I have 100 people on my team and I can get them to work one hour each, that's 100 hours. I can work one hour, and it adds up to 101 hours! Leverage—it's out of all proportion if you use it right.

3. Don't let interest work against you.

Let it work for you. Understand interest, debt and amortization. Read the books I've recommended and apply the principles. Avoid getting a 30-year mortgage. If you already have one, make extra payments whenever you can. A 15-year note will save you a FORTUNE in interest.

4. Pay every penny of tax that's due –just don't leave a tip.

I am not a tax avoider. I am a taxpayer. I gladly pay my fair share of the tax that's due, but I don't want to pay any more than I have to—and that's why owning your own business is so important. Most people leave way too much on the table, and it's because they're employees. There are many creative and honest ways as a business owner and as a direct-selling professional to minimize your tax burden. Taxes are the single largest expense that you're ever going to have. It makes sense to minimize the bill—and you can.

5. Give away a portion of your income every time you are paid.

Pay yourself, but pay God too. You need to get in the habit of giving. Whether it's a tenth to your church for tithing or to any good cause or charity, you will always find greater abundance in giving. No matter what level you can give, you will get more back as a result of giving, because your money doesn't own you. Karen and I have always given 10 to 20 percent of our income back in tithing, to the community, to people in need, or to causes we get behind. There were times early in our marriage where had to ask ourselves, "Do we pay our tithing or do we buy groceries?" We paid our tithing.

It's truth followed by the application of truth that ultimately matters. It's important to know financial principles, but it's what you do with what you know that counts. So many Americans today aren't financially literate enough to know that the deck is stacked against them. These five basic principles can make all of the difference.

In my research for this book on the different generations, I was struck that money is the primary concern for all three of the generational groups I address in this book. So here are some thoughts for you:

APPLICATION

Boomers and Financial Wellness

The good news for Boomers is that they will live longer than any generation in history. That's also bad news because they risk running out of money long before they run out of life. Pensions have mostly disappeared and Social Security most likely faces eventual cuts. Only half of Boomers have saved more than $100,000 for their retirement, which could be easily eaten up in just a few years, especially if there are health problems. All of this together means a harsh outlook for many Boomers.

Financial wellness for Boomers may very well depend on just working longer. Ten more years of savings at a higher rate of income could mean the difference between poverty and wellness. Fortunately, if you're a Boomer, you're probably healthy enough to continue working for a few more years, and you might find it more rewarding anyway, than retiring to an unproductive sort of life.

Also, you can contribute the maximum to a 401K-style account and cut your expenses to eliminate as much debt as possible. This only makes sense.

However, it's not too late to start your own business. A retired brain is still full of priceless knowledge that younger brains don't have. Cash in on your years of experience and become a consultant—many of them make a lot of money from doing just a few projects a year.

Franchising and direct selling are great ways for senior Boomers to pick up a lot of extra money, stay active, and contribute to their social wellness at the same time. It can also be fun. If you own a home, you can make it pay by putting it on AirBnB a few weeks a year while you vacation. Finally, get out of the house: All you need to drive for Uber is a cell phone and a car. There are many ways to supplement your income in retirement that you might not have even considered.

Gen Xers and Financial Wellness

As we've noted, Gen X is the "Worried Generation"—with worries about their jobs and their financial future. They have loans for their education to pay off as well as saving for their children's education.

Finally, they worry about their own retirement. All of this produces incredible financial stress.

The good news is that most of them still have time to get themselves on track financially. If you're a Gen Xer, you can start your own "Plan B" business. You can contribute a percentage point or two more to your retirement Plan and automatically escalate it over time. Blast your debt: find a few dollars a day that you can cut from your expenses and put them toward your debts. Those payments will add up gradually, but in the end will save you a fortune in interest.

Millennials and Financial Wellness

I came across a statement from a Millennial who said that nothing in her college education prepared her to manage her money. Imagine that! She has a degree, but no idea how to take control of her financial life. Still, Millennials are learning fast—and the principles from this chapter are exactly what they need.

Fortunately, they live in a period where they can take more control of their financial future than any generation in the past. Contributing to a 401K now will pay off big for them over time. Time is their greatest asset. They can put time to work for them by saving now and letting compound interest work for them instead of against them. They seem quite aware that Social Security might not be for them what it has been for earlier generations, so a lot of them are making good decisions: 82 percent of them are regularly investing money in their future (if only their parents had done that).

They are also more likely to start and own a business than their older counterparts, which promises them more financial independence. The financial future of Millennials can be bright if they will follow the advice in this book.

INTELLECTUAL WELLNESS

A mind stretched by a new idea can never regain its original dimension.

- Oliver Wendell Holmes Jr.

Intellectual wellness means nonstop learning. Learning makes you not only useful to your team and your customers, but also interesting and exciting. You can't really call yourself a "well person" if your mind is empty or full of dusty old ideas long past their usefulness.

In my early jobs I was always the young sales guy that kept saying, "Can I go to the FranklinCovey seminars? Can I go to Language of Selling? Can I go to Karrass Negotiation? Can I go to hear Tony Robbins? Will the company pay for it?" I consistently wanted to learn more.

One of my greatest learning moments was when I was on sales calls to Nu Skin and I had a buyer named Wes, who was a supply chain manager. I remember trying to figure out how I was going to sell him on our business. I found out that he was a great student of business books, easily digesting a couple of books a month. I thought, "How can this guy have the time to read that much when he's so busy with his job?" But he turned me onto this thing called Audio Book Summaries, these little audio segments that function like the Cliff Notes version of a book.

I was captivated by this idea and started devouring audio books myself. Both Wes and I listened to the same ones. You could almost call us a book club! In our weekly meetings, I wasn't even talking about what services we could offer. It was simply, "What was your insight from chapter one of that book? Wasn't that interesting?" This was how I built my relationship with him. I resonated with him on a different level than any other vendor could, and the business naturally came my way.

I'm constantly digesting and learning from an audiobook. You talk about fun; this is what I do with my spare time. This is what I do. When I'm mowing the lawn, I'm listening to books. When I'm multi-tasking on a plane, I'm listening to books. When I'm in my car, I don't listen to the radio, I listen to books.

One of the programs I loved was John Cummuta's *Debt-Free and Prosperous Living*. It was during this time that my father was suffering from an advanced stage of cancer, and we knew he didn't have long to live. I brought the CDs home to share with him when he was bed-ridden and really slowing down. The book seemed to energize him. He pulled out his yellow legal pad that he was fond of and did some calculations. After a few minutes I realized he was making a kind of financial record of his adult life—and comparing it to what it could have been.

"Look," he said when he was done. "If I had done the things in this book when I was your age, imagine where I'd be today. Promise me, Son. Promise me you won't make the same mistakes."

Well, I don't think my dad made many mistakes in his life, and he did what seemed best to him. But it's true—anyone who learns the basics of prosperous living early in life and then applies them will transform their future. In my chapter on financial wellness, I shared what I learned then, and I'll share what I have learned since.

My point in this chapter is that nonstop learning is absolutely necessary to your wellness. Anyone who decides to stop studying and learning, fails in that very moment.

I honestly don't believe that any leader today can lead an organization without constantly learning. A college degree is incredibly valuable. I didn't get that degree, and I actually lost one of my corporate jobs over it. I was making the biggest money I'd ever made, but I had to walk away from that job because the HR department said, "If you didn't graduate with your degree, you're off the wage scale." I was delivering $50 million in a new division of revenue to them, but they were still insisting I finish my education. It was that important to them. So think again if you think college is not for you.

But even if you're not going to get a university education, you must constantly be educating yourself. You might want to get continuing education credits. In my case, I took classes at the University of Utah, BYU, and the University of Phoenix. But those classes were not my only education. Just as important to me was ongoing learning from Nightingale-Conant, FranklinCovey seminars, Karrass Negotiation, and many others. I found great mentors in those audio book summaries. Eventually I bought the entire CD library of summaries, and I think I've probably digested 1,000 books on every topic through that system. I never would have had time to do that if I had had to read every word. (Frankly, it makes my brain hurt to think I did that!)

Every commute, driving on the 405 in California for hours every day back and forth, I was able to learn from these great authors. To me, it wasn't a matter of just taking in one particular thing or trying to find shortcuts to the skills I needed. I learned a tremendous amount that just made me a wiser and more thoughtful person.

I definitely feel like I've gained sort of a Ph.D. in the best business thinking from listening over the years to all the authors of all these books, all of the perspectives. I've read entire biographies of Jack Welch and Steve Jobs and Elon Musk and other great CEOs. I've digested what they did. I don't know how many MBA students do that. A friend who teaches in the MBA program of a major university tells me that his students do not read very much at all. They really don't know what these great writers have to say. All I know is that my own study has turned me on to a whole different level of thinking.

Think of your network as a learning network.

About two thirds of American adults are active on Facebook, and about a third of those get their news from it. Interestingly, though, they don't think of it as a news site, but as a way to connect with their friends. For them, Facebook becomes a learning site. Almost 60 percent of Facebook users share articles with their networks because they're interested in what they learn from them.

A lot of people in your network, maybe most, are hungry to learn. They want to improve their lives. They want great ideas about how to grow their business. They want to hear how others have faced and overcome the thorny challenges of succeeding in the direct-selling business. Many just want to discover new things and enjoy learning.

When you make your network a book group or a learning network, you help them in several ways.

- They learn from each other ideas to help the business.

- They discover ways of helping each other.

- Brainteasers are fun and create competition.

- People in the network bond faster and better.

Also, a learning network gives you the opportunity to do what big, successful companies do—"content marketing."

Content marketing is different from advertising, which is one-way communication. Content marketing is about sharing information, articles, videos, and social media posts that get people talking. The idea is to create a conversation—to stimulate interest in your products.

The thing I love about content marketing is not just that it builds the business but that it builds knowledge and relationships. My friendship with Wes meant more to me than just the fact that he bought from me. We really enjoyed each other's insights. I learned a lot of lessons from Wes. I gained a friend, and learning is a lot more fun and useful when it's shared.

Early on in my career I came to understand that whatever I didn't know, I could learn. I don't have a college degree to hang on the wall. But I feel like I got my degree from all of the reading and studying I have done since leaving college. The truth is, I'd rather have the wisdom that comes from in-the-trenches personal development books than what comes from most university courses anyway. The wisdom of personal development books is far more interesting and far more applicable to one's everyday life.

I always have my nose in a book or am listening to an audiobook. I can't get enough. People ask what books I recommend. A short list of books I have recently studied is below:

- *Lead the Field* – Earl Nightingale (I listen to this every 90 days!)

- *Financial Peace University* - Dave Ramsey

- *The Monk Who Sold His Ferrari* - Robin Sharma

- *Awaken the Giant Within* - Tony Robbins

- *Debt-Free & Prosperous Living* - John Cummuta,

- *Rich Dad Poor Dad* - Robert Kiyosaki

- *No Money Down* - Carlton Sheets

- *Multiple Streams of Income* - Robert Allen

- *Mindset* – Carol Dweck

- *Essentialism* - Greg McKeown

- *The Seven Habits of Highly Effective People* – Stephen R Covey

- *What Do You Say When You Talk to Yourself* – Shad Helmstetter

- *Titan* – The Life of John D Rockefeller - Ron Chernow

- *Onward, How Starbucks Fought Their Way Back* - Howard Schultz.

- *Unshakable* – Tony Robbins

- *The Upstarts: How Uber, AirBnB, and the Killer Companies of the New Silicon Valley Are Changing the World* – Brad Stone

- *Tools of Titans* – Timothy Ferris

- The CEO library audio series

- Biographies on Jack Welch, Steve Jobs and Elon Musk

When I have personal or business issues to solve, I start searching my mind. I ask myself, "Where have I read about a situation like this before? Who went through a similar challenge?" Whether it was a biography, or the implementation of business tactics explained in a Harvard Business Review report, or an Executive Book Summary, chances are I have come across something similar in my studies. That's why continual reading is so important. Most of our challenges in life have already been worked on by someone who is smarter or wiser than most of us. One might as well use their experience and ingenuity to tackle the problems.

Most books that I have are books that either I sought out because I wanted to know more on the subject, or books that were recommended by a respected acquaintance, or are based on previous books I have read or listened to. The recommendations from Audible are great. It sees the books I've read and then make recommendations based on other authors who have written on similar topics. Just yesterday, my brother told me about an amazing book that he just completed. I always note those recommendations in my notebook or on my phone. I will take down the name of the book, the author, and make a note of the person who recommended it. I will look it up on Audible and I'll buy it. Whether I read it immediately or not, it doesn't matter. It's now in my library. Every book has a few gold nuggets that I can extract and use.

I firmly believe that we move towards and become like the people we hang around. Reading books and listening to audio books are ways to vicariously hang around people that we cannot be with, either because they have passed on, or because we don't know them personally. If I ever need an emotional pick-me-up, I have three or four key books that always do the job.

Number one, far and away, *Lead the Field*, by Earl Nightingale. For whatever reason, Earl Nightingale has a calming, inspiring effect on me whenever I hear his voice; I want to be a better person. I listened to him as a kid, and his voice and his words resonated with me. He was an incredible person. What I like about Earl Nightingale is there's no hidden agenda. His stuff is timeless and powerful. His audio, *The Greatest Secret* is a gold mine. His *Lead the Field* is incredible. Every chapter has an impactful story, and it begins with a principle and builds to the next. I try to listen to it every 90 days.

Number two, I get that same feeling from Tony Robbins when he talks about passion and focus and growth. He's made a business of motivating people, and that's fantastic. I hope to do the same someday.

Stephen Covey is another one. I was fortunate enough to have him as a personal mentor, and was honored to be interviewed by him personally, and featured in one of his Seven Habits books. I need the constant reminder of his Seven Habits, and I love what he teaches. I love everything about what the Seven Habit principles stand for. They're timeless.

Like Nightingale, here's a man who has passed on, but his teachings continue to impact people everywhere.

Jim Rohn is another guide who I love, who is no longer with us. For those building a direct selling business, his audio program, *Building Your Network Marketing Business* is a masterpiece. A few year's ago I decided that I wouldn't let a day go by without listening to it. I literally made it a habit to listen to it every single day for an entire year. There were times when I would listen to it two or three times on repeat in my car. I could almost quote it word for word. It made a great difference to my thinking and how I treat others.

APPLICATION
Boomers and Intellectual Wellness

Baby Boomers were taught in a linear fashion. They read books, often from cover to cover. Lecturers using overhead projectors, filmstrips, and some video taught them. Boomers used mimeograph machines and slide rules.

Most Baby Boomers, always looking for self-fulfillment, are not going to retire to the golf course. Many of them are going back to school, even moving close to universities so they can take the classes they've always wanted to take. So-called "university-based retirement communities (UBRCs)" are popping up everywhere. Older Boomers "want active, intellectually stimulating environments."[xii]

If you're a Boomer you might love the idea of a learning-centered retirement community. But with the amazing opportunities technology provides for learning, you don't have to move at all. Think of the possibilities: audiobooks, podcasts, TED talks—there's a treasure trove of learning out there.

With your long experience, you might also get excited about teaching what you know. It's so easy to set up your own YouTube channel and offer to the world the lessons you've learned in your life.

Gen Xers and Intellectual Wellness

At school, Gen Xers were taught in pods or modules. They were the last generation to use encyclopedias. They learned in a structured environment that included some lecture and small group activities. They are the only generation in which fewer of them went to college than their parents did.

Gen Xers are intrinsic learners who view learning as an independent, self-directed activity. Many don't read books, but prefer to learn by listening rather than reading. In the classroom they are self-motivated, provided that they see the learning as relevant. They place greater value on work-life balance and fun than did their workaholic parents. WIIFM (what's in it for me?) is their motto when it comes to learning. They can be somewhat impulsive and impatient in groups and prefer to be given lots of discretion, yet they often crave individual attention and feedback. If you are a Gen Xer, get the Audible app and grab a platinum membership to start listening to two good books a month. Start with the ones on this list found in this chapter.

Millennials and Intellectual Wellness

Millennials learn in a networked structure. When asked to investigate a topic they turn to the Internet. Many wonder why anyone would read a book. They are the first generation of digital natives. Their learning environment is very flexible. They have always had access to unlimited amounts of information available at their fingertips and are comfortable changing focus quickly. Their whiteboard is the iPad.

Millennials crave new and meaningful experiences. As one expert says, "Millennials love learning. According to a recent study by PWC, Millennials actually ranked training and development as the most highly valued employee benefit. They have a mindset of continuous learning and knowledge consumption, and are eager to access information when and where they need it."[xiii]

If you are a Millennial or have them on your team, make learning a big part of your life. Just about everything you know will probably be obsolete in a year or two anyway. Turn your interactions with your team and your customers into "learning conversations" and I'll bet your business naturally grows.

And while you're at it, turn your commute into an opportunity to learn as well. Put your favorite playlist on hold this month. Try instead listening to learn by using Audible and listen to *Lead The Field*. Even if it's just a chapter a day.

OCCUPATIONAL WELLNESS

Start a part-time business and make as many mistakes as you possibly can while you still have your daytime job.

– Robert Kiyosaki

When I was a young teenager, through no fault of his own, my dad lost his job. He could have kept it if he was willing to relocate to California, but as a family, we loved where we lived and decided against it. It was a stressful time for us. Dad did many things right, but to his continual bewilderment, managing money was not one of them. In true Boomer fashion, my mom didn't work outside the home. Dad's bi-weekly paycheck was all the money that we had. When his company left the state, my dad saw his "Plan A" career disappear, and he had no backup.

Back then, the man in the home got a job with a good company, contributed to the retirement plan, and stayed with it until he quit working. For my dad, losing his job changed everything, especially how he looked at life. It also had a profound effect on my attitude about what I was going to do with my career.

What was so devastating at the time turned out to be a great blessing. Dad quickly found a better job with better pay as vice president of a very cool nutritional manufacturing business. I worked there in the summers and eventually full-time with my dad in the sales department.

It's amazing how often the things that we think are so bad when they happen turn out to be just the opposite.

As a result of that experience, Dad always promoted the idea of having career and a "Plan B." "Don't ever rely on a job. Make sure that a "Plan B" always backs up your job'" my dad would tell us kids. I took his counsel seriously. Throughout my high school years I owned a landscape business, a window washing business, and was a DJ - I did dances on the weekends. I sold Sony Walkmans, headsets, and CD players. I worked summers throwing bags in blenders where my dad worked. Sometimes I had three businesses going on at once—while I was going to school!

When I got to college, I needed a better job, so I made a proposal to my dad to work at his company. He took me seriously and got me a cold-calling job in the sales department. It was the lowest job on the totem pole, but I was grateful to have it. And I was good at it. I realized that I could make money working for someone else.

That was okay for a while. I was learning and growing and having great experiences that were critical for my career and my life. These were the kinds of lessons that I could best learn working with others who had already been down the road. I had the opportunity to spend the better part of six years working with my dad. I wouldn't trade that time for all of the money in the world.

Over time though, I came to understand that the bigger opportunities come from having one's own business, even if that business starts out as a "Plan B"—as most businesses do.

If you want to be financially independent at some point, you need a "Plan B" to own your own business. If you don't do that, it will be very difficult to become financially free. I realized that I would have to own a profitable business to make the kind of money I needed to fulfill the dreams I had in mind. Fortunately, I came to that understanding at a very early age.

While still working with my dad, I decided to get my real-estate license. I didn't want to be a real-estate agent—I just wanted the knowledge. I had read Robert Kiyosaki's *Rich Dad Poor Dad*, all about making money in real estate, and also *No Money Down* by Carleton Sheets. I wanted to create some capital by becoming a "no-money-down" investor in real estate. And I did!

After getting my license, I bought a little house and put renters in it. I banked the commission that would otherwise have gone to realtors, and I learned how to cash flow the property. Then I did it again and again. And it worked! I was getting ready for Plan B to become Plan A.

Most of the time, people stay "unfree" in a job because of fear, or they feel that they lack the skills necessary to start their own business. But if you learn how to be a business owner, even if it's in a small business that starts with the basics, you will develop a business owner's mindset. For me it was an easy transition. Owning a direct-selling business is an ideal "Plan B" because you're strategizing, marketing, selling, and dealing with so many of those basics of being a small business owner without taking a great deal of risk.

As I explain in the finance chapter, there are all sorts of benefits to having your own business, even if it's your "Plan B" business. One of the coolest reasons: The legitimate tax benefits that you can enjoy. Business expenses are taxed differently from other kinds of expenses. It's not about cheating on your taxes, not about finding ways to not pay your fair share—it's about paying what is due without leaving a tip. Your single biggest expense in life will be income tax. The lowest-cost business that I'm aware of for leveraging those tax-saving benefits is a direct selling business.

In the USA, home-based business owners (i.e., direct sellers) enjoy a host of business tax deductions that some other businesses don't have. There are roughly 137 IRS-approved tax deduction strategies that most people don't know anything about. The list below is just an example of what a home-based business owner may write off:

- Business meals

- Travel

- Education and training

- Entertainment

- Gifting: giving away gifts.

- Online work: spending business-related time online

- Certain out-of-pocket medical, health, dental, vision, and insurance expenses.

When I learned about these tax savings from Robert Kiyosaki's book, I immediately decided to become the owner of my own business, no matter how small the business was going to be. I had no idea how early that opportunity would come.

A turning point came when the company I was working for decided to go in a different direction and was going to cut off some of my most valuable customers and client relationships. I needed to find a new home for them. I always believed in writing my goals, and over the years I had written down this goal perhaps a thousand times: "I will own a $10 million supplement manufacturing company that nets a million dollars a year."

I knew one day that I would do it, and when my company changed direction, I decided to leave the safe, secure job and the guaranteed paycheck and start my own business. It was thrilling and frightening at the same time. We had to second mortgage our house and borrow against everything we had of any value. We put everything on the line. But it turned out to be one of the best decisions we have ever made.

My dad lived in a world in which he expected his career to end in the same company where it began. Today the world is very different. The U.S. Bureau of Labor Statistics has reported on the number of times people in today's marketplace change jobs, on average, 11.7 times.[xiv] Why do they change? Bad bosses? Uninteresting work? Not enough pay?

Most people don't change jobs for any of these reasons. The number-one reason people change jobs, according to a survey of more than 10,000 people, is for more altruistic reasons - to advance their careers and to fulfill a greater purpose. Fundamentally, job switchers leave for work that offers a chance to grow, and to use more of their potential.[xv]

We live in a world that is often void of meaning. The human soul has a need to do things that make a difference. Consider the latest survey findings from a recent New York Times article on why many hate their jobs. The survey, which reached more than 12,000 employees across a broad range of companies and industries, found that 50% lack meaning and significance at work.[xvi]

I believe people should take the time to identify what they are passionate about, and then look for ways to turn that passion into a "Plan B" home-based business.

Let me share a quick story about my mom, who in every way was equal to my dad in character, in ability, and in making me who I am. She was a Baby Boomer mother, who, after the kids were raised, went through what many Boomer moms did, saying, "There's got to be more to life than cleaning, cooking, and changing diapers." She wanted some different experiences, so while my dad was still healthy, she started a pro shop at a tennis club. As things go, someone came into the shop with a network-marketing product. Eventually, she started her own network-marketing business and made a great success of it.

On her office wall hung a picture of a Mercedes Benz SL550 coupe, a car she had always dreamed about. As the mom of five kids, she had always driven a minivan. More than anything, she wanted a cool two-seater to drive with the wind in her hair and without five kids screaming in the back. That was her vision. I'll never forget the day that she earned the car allowance that would cover the cost of that Mercedes she wanted so badly. She was so thrilled! She had the car on order and went down to pick it up. We were so excited for her.

But when she returned, she wasn't in the Mercedes. She drove up in a brand new custom van, pulling a fancy ski boat, and said with tears in her eyes, "I still believe in your kids' dreams, too. I know you will enjoy this boat more than I would have enjoyed that car." That was a cool day! I loved my mom, and I became a believer in direct selling that day.

That experience affected me in a major way. It changed my beliefs. I thought that if my mom could do it, that maybe I could do it too. I realized that there was something about the income leverage and people development that direct selling provides that a regular job does not come close to providing.

When my dad passed away, my mom's "Plan B" business became her Plan A. The residual income from her direct selling business carried her through the most difficult time in her life. Thank heavens my mom had a "Plan B".

APPLICATION

Baby Boomers and Occupational Wellness

Most Boomers are about to enter a "second life"—an extended period of years of good health and vitality but without the need to work for a living. Yet they don't want to stop working because of the social and financial benefits.

The fun thing about upcoming retirement for Baby Boomers is the "Gig Economy." It used to be about delivering pizza or welcoming people at Wal-Mart. Now it's a far richer and more interesting prospect for Boomers as they reach retirement age.

The Gig Economy is a world of projects that you can do on your own time and at your own pace, as much or as little as you want. Take advantage of all that experience and wisdom you gained over decades in your profession. Businesses want on-demand teachers, lawyers, accountants, insurance experts, and especially consultants.

Direct selling is perfect for downshifting Baby Boomers. When you find a product or service you really believe in and gather a group around you of fellow believers, there's no limit to what you can contribute and the money you can make.

Gen Xers and Occupational Wellness

Your parents' formula "Go to school, get a good job, and live happily ever after" hasn't worked out for you so well. You came of age when companies were backing off from all the old job securities. You've had to compete for jobs in a tough marketplace. The old Boomers won't get out of the way and the Millennials are breathing hard behind you, many of them willing to work for nothing just to get experience.

Maybe it's time for "Plan B" - to own your business, even if it's just for a cushion to fall back on in case things don't work out as well as you'd hoped on the job. Besides, by owning your own business, you can build your own dreams instead of someone else's. Succeeding is tough, but starting isn't.

Direct Selling provides a wonderful "Plan B". A good product and a good team can fill so many of your needs—purpose, a great social network, an outlet for your creative side that you can't necessarily get working for someone else.

Millennials and Occupational Wellness

Everyone knows that Millennials are starting a new kind of economy.

The old principles are still vitally important—customers, great products and services, profitability—but there are infinite exciting new ways to practice those principles.

For Millennials, work has to have a high purpose. The money isn't as important to them as having meaningful work and making a contribution. This fact is highlighted in every article I've ever read about Millennials.

The great opportunity for you as a Millennial, then, is to become an independent contractor for life—"Me Inc."—your own brand, your own unique business, serving your own unique purpose. So many of the old barriers to entry fall down with the rise of the Internet.

Direct selling is a natural way for Millennials to express themselves and create their own ideal business. They are the most socially connected generation in human history. They don't get told when to get up, go to work, and what to do with their time. But they are driven, passionate, and hardworking. In other words, they have all the characteristics necessary to make a big success in direct selling. Look for a direct selling company with products you can get passionate about and a cause that gives back in a purposeful way.

PHYSICAL WELLNESS

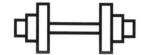

Take care of your body. It's the only place you have to live.

– Jim Rohn

ere's some startling information: The United States spends more money on health care than any other country in the world—around $8,700 per person each year. That's more than double the average of the 34 countries that make up the OECD (the Organization for Economic Cooperation and Development), and far more than second place Switzerland, which spends about $6,300 per year per person. Canada is number ten in the world, spending about $4,400 per year per person.[xvii]

Despite the high spending, Americans are not anywhere near the world's healthiest people. According to research done by the United Nations, Iceland and Sweden take the top spots, while the U.S. comes in at a pathetic 28th out of 188 nations. The U.S. receives its lowest marks in the categories for deaths related to natural disasters, HIV, suicide, and overall violence. More than 35% of Americans are obese, one of the highest levels in the world. The U.S. ranks 64th in the maternal death rate category for every 100,000 births, and 40th in the childhood death rate for children under the age of five.[xviii]

With all of the great things that we have going for us in the USA, this situation just doesn't make sense. What is going on? What are we doing to ourselves?

Maybe there's a better way.

I had a grandpa who was all about natural health. He was a student of reflexology, which he did on our feet on Sunday afternoons. He'd have us put our socks on, massage our feet with the massager, and then do reflexology. He wasn't a doctor, he was a city commissioner—but he believed in natural healing and in organic nutrition long before it was popular. From him I developed an understanding of how important it is to take care of my body, and that there are great ways to do it besides just going to the doctor. My grandpa was born a couple of generations too soon!

As I've explained, my dad was vice president of a cool company that made high quality nutritional products for body builders and athletes. I got deeply interested in it because I loved my dad and wanted to follow in his footsteps, and also because of what I had been taught by my grandfather. I was into nutrition. I did a deep dive into health products and learned what really works to keep people healthy. I learned about the differences between Eastern and Western philosophies of health and came to appreciate the idea of staying well, rather than fixing problems after they arise. I attended trade shows and symposiums. For a few years, I couldn't get enough of it. I loved learning about wellness.

As I explain in the spiritual chapter of this book, when I was 19 years old I was diagnosed with Crohn's colitis and got very sick. The doctors gave me medication to relieve the symptoms, but it turned me into a zombie. So I chose a more natural route. It made a huge difference. I learned that I could manage the disease through my thinking, my physical behavior, and my food choices. I learned then that with proper nutrition, I could manage my health myself much better than the medications could.

I absolutely believe that physical wellness begins with nutrition, even more so than with exercise. Ever since I've been on this path I have not been on any medication and I'm doing great. I don't take antibiotics. I take a massive dose of flavonoids every day. I go to the health food store and I buy the highest quality products I can find—no matter who sells them. I'm not fanatical about it, but I definitely try to use the best there is. I actually buy a number of products from direct selling companies because of the quality that I know they deliver. Having been on the manufacturing side of the businesses, I know which companies make the best products. For the most part, the products of reputable network-marketing companies are worth every penny that they cost.

A few years back I was analyzed for food-sensitivity. They took some blood, sent it to a lab, and a few weeks later they told me about every allergen in my system, along with the foods that are good for me and those that I should avoid. I figured that if I was going to live for a while, I wanted to be at my best. I really wanted to know this information. So I now have a comprehensive list of additives in food and medications to avoid. I now know which foods to enjoy. Discovering the foods that work best for me has made an incredible difference as to how I feel. For the rest of my life, I'll be grateful I took that test.

Even without a test like that, your body will pretty much tell you what's right and wrong if you'll listen to it. It helps a lot if you record what your body tells you. I believe there is magic in journaling—in keeping track of what I'm doing with my health. I use a simple little app called "MyFitnessPal," where I can log my meals and track my exercise. It is awesome.

This concept of paying attention and recording things is incredibly useful. I learned from my time-management courses that if I tracked my time for 30 days, I would become aware of how I was spending my time. It's the same thing with money management; half the battle of financial success is knowing where your money goes. Likewise, half the battle of nutrition is becoming aware of what you're eating to the point of tracking it.

You don't have to do it forever. I did it for 30 days and I learned so much. I became aware of what I was eating—both good and bad. I logged every drink I drank. I logged everything. If you start tracking everything you put in your mouth, you'll realize how far off you really are from the healthy food habits you should be forming.

We don't learn from experience, said John Dewey. We learn from reflecting on experience, and the only way to learn is through paying attention. If you watch carefully what you eat for just a while, it will become a habit. And changing your food choices doesn't need to be dramatic—often just weaning yourself from a few little things that are corrupting your physical wellness can make a huge difference.

Track what you eat for 30 days. Don't change anything about your diet yet; just track it, even if it's just on a piece of paper or a notepad. Of course, there are apps now that will scan the UPC on any package you pull from the fridge. It will identify the product and ask, "How much did you eat?" The app does all the tracking for you. So it's getting easier and easier to document your food choices and make those little adjustments that will add to your physical wellness.

So I now have a red, yellow, and green list of what foods I should be eating and which ones I need to avoid—including some of my favorite foods that I always ate but I regretted later, foods like watermelon. I had no idea my body doesn't tolerate watermelon very well. And walnuts. Who would have thought? And cucumbers were on this list. And lobster, one of my favorite foods of all time, I have to avoid because it's on my red list of do not eat. By avoiding those foods I feel so much better all of the time.

Now, if nutrition is 90% of your physical wellness, let's see what we can do about the other 10%--exercise.

I've worked for Joe Weider, the legendary trainer of Arnold Schwarzenegger, and I've worked for Bill Philips, the developer of Body for Life. I've worked for some of the best fitness minds in the world, and I followed their systems. I had a personal trainer that came to the house three days a week and kicked my butt. But you know what? Better than all of those systems, at least for me, is one thing that I do—just a simple thing that anybody can do.

It's push-ups!

I got the idea one day when I was waiting for the shower to heat up in the morning. I had two or three minutes to kill, and rather than just stand around thinking, I decided to get down on the floor and do some push-ups. I started out with ten push-ups and then I got in the shower. The next day it was 11 and then I got in the shower. The next day it was

12. In time I got up to 50, 60, 70 push-ups. Because I was just adding one a day, I was gradually getting stronger and stronger and stronger. So cool!

Now I do push-ups every day and am in as good of shape as I have ever been in. Anybody can do that. If not push-ups do sit-ups. I don't care if you're 100 pounds overweight. It doesn't matter. Start with whatever you can do, and do one. Tomorrow do two, and the next day do three.

Pretty soon, you'll figure that if you do a little more each day—one more push up, one more sprint, one more step—after about 30 to 40 days you'll be doing dozens of push-ups where just weeks earlier, you could barely do one. It works with any exercise, jogging included—do just a little more today than you did yesterday.

On day one, maybe all you can do is lace up your shoes. Tomorrow you lace up your shoes and go for a short walk. The next day you lace up your shoes, go for a walk, and put a little jog to it. But you don't need to go out and kill yourself on the first day and then call it quits. Pace yourself. Enjoy the journey. See what a difference it makes in your life!

APPLICATION

Boomers and Physical Wellness

Many Baby Boomers are the richest, most physically active people at their age in history. Fortunately, many are getting into fitness even more in order to stave off the decline of old age. They are doing everything from yoga to triathlon training, and that's great. They are into gyms, personal trainers, and long-term fitness.

Still, too many are choosing a sedentary old age, which comes with hospitals, surgeries, and chronic disease. They are "older, sicker, and fatter" than their parents' generation.

If you're a Baby Boomer, you'll want to maintain what's called "functional fitness," so you can go about your daily life with energy and without being hindered by health problems. You can keep yourself functionally fit by doing relatively few things every day—a short walk, a few pushups, or moderate weightlifting.

Gen Xers and Physical Wellness

Gen Xers have a reputation for being "slackers," but that's unfair. Many Gen Xers have embraced fitness. During the 1990s, they started the gym craze, and CrossFit and other trends originated with Gen X enthusiasm. Now, the aerobics movement has given way to spin classes, hot yoga, interval training, and other activities that are more intense and engaging.

Gen Xers want to work together to get fit in a no-nonsense way. They want to invest less time in a smarter way into maintaining fitness.

Still, two-thirds of Gen Xers could be doing much better at diet, maintaining healthy weight, and exercising. Stress is a serious challenge for them.

If you're a Gen Xer with a heavy schedule, you'll like the observations in this chapter. Keep it simple but be consistent. You owe it to yourself to do what you can to stave off stress and the physical decline that comes with aging.

Start doing those push ups today.

Millennials and Physical Wellness

Millennials don't want to do things that have been done before. They want to find their own way to physical wellness. They are the first group that is perfectly aware of the dangers of an unhealthy, sedentary lifestyle, so many of them are intentionally choosing "wellness."

They use fitness apps and wearable technology to track their progress in things like calories, breathing, steps, and heart rate. They go for group physical activities that are less about competition than about making friends. They are less about looking good and more about feeling holistically well. They are less interested in gyms than in fun runs or at-home fitness workouts.

In other words, Millennials have a very healthy outlook on health—but the great challenge is to tear themselves away from their screens long enough to practice what they believe. Short, intense workouts probably work best for them.

SOCIAL WELLNESS

Tweet others the way you want to be tweeted.

– Germany Kent

One of the most important things I learned from my dad was not something that he sat down and taught me. He didn't explain it to me. He didn't give me a book to read or an audio to listen to.

Instead, it was what I observed and experienced being his son and working with him in business for six years. He always treated others— his family, his neighbors, his friends, and his professional contacts with kindness, with genuine respect, and with unending positivity. He was a man of great social wellness.

It was a great experience to work with him for six years and watch him interact with people. Although he's been gone for over twenty years, I regularly talk with people who knew and loved him. Just the other day someone asked me if I were Paul Reynolds's son and told me how much he had liked my dad. It happens all the time.

Dad was genuinely interested in others and made them feel special. It wasn't phony. It came from the center of his core. He was as authentic a person as anyone I have ever known. My dad was a great friend, not only to me but also to many others.

Research validates that close friends and social connections do wonders for our health and wellness. One study found that people who don't have friends they can identify with or rely on are 50 percent more likely to die prematurely than people with close friends and strong social ties.[xix] Low social wellness compares to other risk factors this way:

- Equivalent to smoking 15 cigarettes a day

- Equivalent to being an alcoholic

- More harmful than not exercising

- Twice as harmful as obesity

The researchers analyzed data from hundreds of previously published studies and determined that friends and family have a significant impact on health for many reasons. The calming touch of another person, meaning in life, a sense of responsibility for others—these and many other social-wellness factors strongly affect physical and mental health. "That sense of purpose and meaning translates to taking better care of themselves and taking fewer risks," one of the researchers said.

Unfortunately, the average person has fewer friends now than a generation ago. According to the General Social Survey,[xx] the number of Americans who say they have no close friends has almost tripled in recent decades. "Zero" is the most common response when people are asked how many confidants they have.

Furthermore, the number of friends is dropping. In 1985, three people were important to the average American adult. Twenty years later that number had dropped to two, and now some research suggests it is less than that.[xxi]

Many say that social media has taken the place of the old intimate social network. Now it's Facebook. It's Instagram. It's Twitter. Supposedly, the average Facebook user has about 338 Facebook friends: but how many of them are really friends? You could pass most of them on the street and not even recognize them. They're not really friends. They're contacts. There's a big, big difference between a friend and a contact.

To a great extent for all three generational groups, but especially for Millennials, social interaction happens on a phone or a laptop. There's little face-to-face contact. Social media let you photo-shop and engineer everything to make things look better than they really are. The social media picture is not authentic.

Your best, most authentic social experience is going to be when you're sitting kneecap to kneecap with a person, where you can look at them and get to know them. Can you use technology to do that? Yes. You can have a Zoom conversation with somebody and see his or her face. You can see their expression. You can hear their enthusiasm. You can catch the social cues. You can catch the nonverbal communication. But it's still not the same.

Understand that although there is a place for technology, it is a distant second to being in the same room with someone. The only way you're going to have an authentic experience with people is to go and see them. Be there. Immerse yourself in their company. Shake their hands. Don't rely on technology to do all of that work. Technology is handy, but it only gets the ball so far down the field. Especially in business, being there can get you to the goal line much better than Zoom or Go-to-Meeting can.

I learned early on from my dad that the best way to do business was not talking on the phone or sending email: it was getting in front of as many people as possible and connecting with them individually. So we'd go to all the trade shows in our industry, meet people, and then jump on a plane or drive to their location so that he could sit with them and talk about doing business. He could get more done in one meeting than with ten phone calls. Trust is developed face to face, and people do business with those that they trust.

One of the turning points in my business career was when the company I was working for decided to go in a different direction and was going to cut off some of my most valuable client relationships. Those relationships meant a lot to me. I needed to find a new home for them and for myself. I left that safe, secure job and started my own business.

I had to find a facility capable of handling our products, and I had heard about a guy named Vance who had a huge warehouse. I found out that he was using only a small part of it and was probably losing his shirt. So I thought, "What if I partnered with this guy and brought my millions of dollars' worth of business to him?" I assumed that Vance lived in Salt Lake City, where the warehouse was located. I found his number and called him to make an appointment for us to meet.

I asked, "Vance, where are you?"

He replied with some curiosity, "Who is this again?"

"I'm Jeremy Reynolds and I have a proposal that I'd like to discuss."

He asked, "Jeremy Reynolds? You wouldn't be related to Paul Reynolds, would you?"

I smiled and said, "I am. That's my dad. How do you know him?"

"He was an amazing individual. I met your dad a few times over the years. He had a competing product that he sold next to my booth at trade shows. He actually inspired me to produce the product that I have today."

And I'm thinking, "You've got to be kidding me."

From that point on, the discussion changed. He loosened up and acted like we were old friends. It's amazing how that happens when trust takes over.

"So what do you need, Jeremy Reynolds?"

I said, "Vance, I'd like to talk to you about a proposal that I have to bring you some business and maybe to do something together."

He says, "Look, as a rule I don't do partnerships. I'm not sure that I'm your right guy. But if you'd like to talk about it, I'd be happy to do the call. Should we do it now?"

I said, "No, I'd like to come to you. I assume that you are here in Salt Lake City?"

He says, "No, I live half the year in Sacramento, California, and I live half the year in Kenai, Alaska. Right now I'm in Alaska."

I said, "I'll be there tomorrow." And I hung up the phone, called Delta, and booked two plane tickets to Alaska, one for me and one for Karen. I really didn't have the money or the time but this was important. Also, I knew that dad was right. You can get more done with a face-to-face meeting than you can with ten phone calls. We traveled to Kenai, Alaska, to convince Vance to be my business partner. There is no way I would have accomplished that on the phone or on the web.

So the next day, after a long flight, we arrived in the tiny regional airport at Kenai, Alaska. I'm dressed in a sport coat and tie, carrying my big, important business bag. Karen's dressed to the hilt, and Vance shows up in his worn, flannel shirt, tattered Levis, and a Suburban with the stuffing coming out of the seats. He laughs at us and suggests that we might be overdressed. (He gave us crap about it many times afterwards.)

I'm thinking maybe I should just get down to business. I said, "You know Vance, I'd like to just dive into this. I mean, we're going to be flying back tomorrow and just wanted to come up to shake your hand and meet you. Could we maybe have a quick discussion at the coffee shop across the street?"

He's like, "No, no, no, no, no. Are you kidding me? You're going to get a good night's rest. Bag your hotel reservation. You're staying at my place. I want you to meet my wife, Elizabeth. We've got a room for you. You're going to stay with us and in the morning, we're going to go fishing. And if we have some time later, then maybe we'll talk business."

I realized that he needed to know who we were before he was ever going to entertain the idea of going into business with us. And there I was, saying, "Let's jump in right here and now." I also realized that the only reason I had the opportunity to meet with him, was the impression that my dad had made on him so many years before.

So I put the business discussion aside, met Elizabeth, and had dinner and a great night's sleep. We got up at 4:30 the next morning and went fishing in one of the most beautiful spots on planet Earth. I thought we were going to drive somewhere to a boat, but we literally walked out his back door, and down to the river where he had everything ready to go. He probably fishes five days a week—just like rabid golfers do where I live in Utah.

I'm sitting there on the Kenai River and wanting so much to get into my presentation, to do the business with him—but I stopped and had an "aha moment." All at once I appreciated that fishing on that incredible river was his passion and that if I was going to do business with him that I'd better love it too—not in an artificial way, but the way my dad would love it—because Vance loved it. That moment changed me. Until that moment, I was so caught up in the business that I came close to missing the boat, so focused on my own needs that I almost blew it.

That afternoon we went back to his home and Vance said, "So tell me about your proposal." I said, "Well, I have a few slides." And he said, "Okay. Well, show it to me." I show it to him. He half-heartedly flipped though the slides, and I'm thinking, he's not into this at all. Finally, he set my presentation aside, looked at me, and said, "We're going fishing again."

And I'm like, "Really?"

"Yeah, we're going out to fish for halibut in the inlet."

I think, "Oh crap, not again,"

But I remembered my epiphany a few hours earlier and adjusted my attitude. We fished for halibut all that afternoon. It was an experience of a lifetime. We caught more halibut than we could have eaten in a year. So we went back to his house where he had a fish-processing unit right in his garage. While he was flash-freezing fish for us to take home, he finally started asking me questions.

"So, you really think we can make this work?"

"Well, yeah, Vance, I really do."

"So you'll run the business."

"Yeah, I'll run the business."

"'Cause I'm not coming to run the business. I live in Alaska and in Sacramento, so you're going to run the business. You're okay with that?"

"Yeah, Vance, I'm okay with that."

He didn't even want to talk about business until he decided if he could trust me, and his way to determine that was to take me fishing. He asked about Karen and me and our family and my dad. That night, over an incredible halibut dinner, he asked, "So, what would this agreement that we'd come up with look like?"

I said, "You know, I don't have it written out but why don't we put something together?"

"Here, write it out on this paper." He pushed me the backside of an envelope.

I proposed a 50/50 partnership and we were near an agreement, but he came up with a little nuance at the very end. "So, who controls?" he asked.

I had no idea at that moment how important that particular question was.

"It's only fair that if we're partners and if one of us were to pass away, how would you propose that to be handled?" he asked.

I said, a little tongue in cheek, "You're a little bit older than I am, so I suppose that if that happens maybe one percent would swing to me."

He says, "Okay, that sounds fair to me. Let's do this." And we shook hands.

What I didn't know was that Vance was, at that very moment, in advanced stage of prostate cancer, just like my dad, and wasn't expected to live much longer. He didn't disclose it in the meeting, but he insisted that I have one percent more of a stake than he did - if he passed.

The most amazing part for me was, I never would have had that business, never would have pivoted my life, none of that would have happened had I not been willing to jump on a plane, go fishing with him, and do what he enjoyed doing most. He needed to know that I was authentic and that I was trustworthy. There's no video-conferencing technology that could have done that. You can't Zoom fishing in the Cook Inlet. You can't effectively FaceTime getting on a boat in the Kenai in his backyard. You can't do it. It's an authentic experience that you have to have face to face.

Now, that's a long way of showing that we need to rekindle relationships with people not only in our business, but also in our lives. We need to be looking at how we can expand our social circle with real live meetings and interactions and experiences.

To me, the greatest thing that we can do is to create experiences that matter—to be in the places and with the people that will make your life as rich as possible—to go beyond anything that you thought possible.

To me, that's what this is all about. Social wellness means that we go and experience the world with others.

APPLICATION
Baby Boomers and Social Wellness

As we've seen, Boomers get emotionally wiser and more balanced as they age. But they also have a tendency to get more and more isolated because so many broke away from traditional family connections years ago: They are the most divorced generation in history. As we've seen social isolation is just as dangerous to their health as smoking or heart disease.

Yet the Boomer generation is the wealthiest, most experienced in history. They could contribute so much to society, but not if they disconnect from the world in their senior years.

So if you're a Boomer, work on building your network. Connect actively with old friends on Facebook or some other medium. Don't move away to Florida or someplace where you don't know a soul. Find ways to keep up the conversation with your loved ones—visiting family, going to church, volunteering, taking classes.

You don't have to turn into the life of the party, but if you value your mental and physical wellness, you need to take your social wellness seriously with just a few simple activities every week.

Gen Xers and Social Wellness

Overscheduled and overstressed, Gen Xers often feel obligated to shut down all of their social activities as non-essentials. They lose contact with the friends of their youth. They stop going out with friends and even their spouse or partner. Work takes over and consumes everything, even vacation time.

It's easy to say, "balance your life." But it isn't easy to do. As a Gen Xer myself, it took me a while to re-learn from Vance (see above) about the importance of just making a human connection. Vance needed to know not only about the business—he needed to know me.

It may take some discipline and planning, but you can't let your career be your life. Schedule time to be with your family and friends. A short walk, an hour on a playground with your kids, an evening out—these things cost nothing compared to the gains you will make for a more meaningful, happier life.

Millennials and Social Wellness

For Millennials, socializing generally means social media. Most have dozens or more Facebook connections, Twitter followings, and so forth. Ironically, Millennials' devotion to social media (some scholars consider it an "addiction") can actually induce depression. It means less face-to-face time with people and less self-reflection. For a large number of Millennials, social media has taken the place of work, family, even eating.

Deep meaningful relationships can't be created through an electronic device. Although there's no problem with social media itself, excess is a real problem. It will take a little discipline for Millennials to put the phone away and talk to the family at dinnertime, go on a date, take a walk with friends, and get to know themselves.

SPIRITUAL WELLNESS

We are not human beings having a spiritual experience, we are spiritual beings having a human experience and Infinite love is the only truth...

- Pema Chodron

Our exploration of the eight dimensions of wellness ends with the spiritual dimension.

This is a book about becoming healthy physically, socially, mentally, emotionally, and spiritually. It is interesting to note that the origin of the words "health," "wholeness," and "holiness" all have the same common root—to be whole or complete. In some respects, a healthy person is also a holy person.

Some people believe you have to be a religious person to be spiritually well. That might or might not be true for you. The word "religion" literally means to be "bound" to a particular belief or creed, which is very different from being whole, or holy. I believe that a person can be holy without being bound to a religious creed. Spirituality is not religion. Although spirituality and religion often go together, they don't have to. For now, we'll leave religion alone and explore the spiritual dimension of wellness.

Spirituality includes a sense of connection to something bigger than yourself. It involves a search for meaning. It is a universal human experience—something that touches us all. People may describe a spiritual experience as sacred or transcendent or as simply a deep sense of being alive, whole, and interconnected with others and with the world. Like your sense of purpose, your personal definition of spirituality will likely change with life's experiences.

As I have explained, I grew up in a good home and community where many of my friends took two years out of their lives to serve missions for their church. It was totally voluntary, and it was okay if you didn't go, but it was something that I wanted to do. In order to qualify, you get interviewed and submit some paperwork and then wait for a letter telling you where and when you are going to serve. I remember the thrill and the anticipation of waiting for that letter to arrive. I was like a kid at Christmas time. I knew I could be sent pretty much anywhere in the world.

When the calling finally came through, I was ecstatic. I was going to Sofia, Bulgaria, and would be one of the first ever to do so! On my own, I immediately started studying the language, the history of the country, and the people. I couldn't have been more excited! But then, as things often do, something happened to change all of my plans.

As I've explained in other chapters, I was diagnosed with Crohn's colitis, a digestive disease that can cause all sorts of problems if not addressed. It's like having canker sores in your intestinal tract. The only thing they could give me at the time was a drug to reduce the inflammation and Zoloft to calm the mind. I hated how the drugs made me feel. I was miserable.

Because of the disease, they reassigned me. Instead of being one of the first to go to Bulgaria, which sounded like such a cool adventure, I was reassigned to stay in the United States instead of exotic Bulgaria. To a 19-year-old kid who really hadn't seen much, it was devastating. I almost chose not to go. And to top if off, the drugs I was taking for the disease made me so sick that I refused to take them anymore. I was miserable and disgusted both physically and spiritually.

About that time I learned about biofeedback therapy, and I decided to give it a try. I met with a wonderful woman who taught me in a number of sessions how to relax using breathing techniques, how to visualize peaceful settings, and how to heal myself with my mind. I was able to stop the drugs, and serve a very successful mission.

I also came to appreciate and understand the incredible healing power of the mind. In many ways it was a spiritual experience. I am grateful for the Crohn's disease because of what I learned about healing as a result. It changed my life for the better. Countless times I have called upon this mental power to heal and to address sickness and stress.

In researching his book *Tools of Titans*, Tim Ferriss interviewed a number of major corporate executives and billionaires to find out about their common traits. One thing struck me: they all seem to find time to meditate—to use the brain to heal the body. Mindfulness is a big trend right now. You can hardly pick up a magazine without finding an article or two on the subject. It's not just on the fringe anymore. It's actually a key strategy that winners use to find spiritual wellness in today's hectic environment.

What is mindfulness? It's probably many things, but in my reading it's about slowing the brain down and getting in tune with the present moment—with the "right now." It's letting go of the past and worries about the future, at least for a little while. I believe it is what I learned to do years ago in order to cope with my mission. M. Scott Peck, a psychologist who wrote much on spirituality and personal growth, penned the following:

> Some Catholics have a concept I very much admire: the Sacrament of the Present Moment. It suggests that every moment of our lives is sacred, and that we should make of each moment a sacrament. Were we to do this we would think of the entire world as diffused with holiness. Wherever we might be would be a holy place for us, and we would see the holy, even sainthood, in everyone we encounter.

It's hard to be mindful—to be aware of the present—if we are worried, stressed, and anxious about the past or the future.

According to Earl Nightingale:

> Let me show you how much time we waste on worrying about the wrong problems. Here's a reliable estimate of the things people worry about. Things that never happen: 40%. Things over and past that can't be changed by all the worry in the world: 30%. Needless worries about our health: 12%. Petty, miscellaneous worries: 10%. Real, legitimate worries: 8%.

In short, 92% of the average person's worries take up valuable time, cause painful stress, even mental anguish, and are absolutely unnecessary.

That observation gives me so much hope: Control what you can control and let go of the rest. Find out where you can make a difference, concentrate your energy there, and let the other stuff go.

My model for addressing real problems is summed up in the acronym **GROW**:

- **G** is for **GOAL**: Set your goal to be as specific as possible.

- **R** is for **REALITY**: Know where you are now and how far you need to go.

- **O** is for **OPTION**: Identify three options that could work to accomplish your goal.

- **W** is for the **WAY FORWARD**: Choose your best option and take action – now!

Whether success takes a minute or a year or many years, if you use the GROW model, you will find it. As Nightingale says, if only eight percent of our worries are real, and only half of those make all the difference . . . My goodness, why don't we GROW the opportunities that matter and forget about all the other worries that get in the way? It's about being proactive in the areas that really matter and letting the other stuff go.

I recently attended a business workshop on the subject of inspiration (imagine that—inspiration in business!). I discovered that the seminar was about many of the same things I had discovered about biofeedback all those years ago. What was new to me was the science about the brain, what goes on when the brain is stressed, and why it is so important to slow down and get to a healthy mental state.

The presenter explained it this way: The brain consists of billions of neurons and synaptic connections. The root of all mental activity, including emotions and behaviors, is electric and chemical communication that takes place between these neurons. When the neurons are working in harmony, they form a synchronized "neural network" linked to a specific state of consciousness. This electrical activity produces "brain waves." Neurologists have identified five categories of brain waves differentiated by how quickly they move or vibrate. From fastest to slowest, they are:

- **Gamma** – super fast

- **Beta** – dominant during awake time

- **Alpha** – day dreaming, resting

- **Theta** – sleeping and dreaming

- **Delta** – deep sleeping

Beta waves dominate our waking hours. These are very fast brain waves that accompany critical thinking, planning, communicating, writing, reading, problem solving, and other hard mental work. Beta waves indicate conscious, logical thought. They also tend to have a stimulating effect on the body. The beta brain is the working brain: it gathers information and gets things done.

However, too much beta activity leads to excessive stress, higher anxiety, and mental burnout. People who worry, who are angry, or who are excessively negative produce a never-ending stream of beta brain waves, which can be very damaging to both mental and physical wellness.

Mindfulness is intentionally slowing the brain down so that it can rest and restore itself so it can operate more efficiently. When we slow our mental activity down, the brain waves transition from beta to alpha, and all sorts of wonderful things happen—we think more clearly, we have more innovative ideas, we're more creative, and we produce more of the right body chemistry. We become happier and less stressed, and we're more open to ways to make a contribution to the world, to be of service to others.

The key is to make a few transitions to a slower brain state throughout the day. Every couple of hours, take a few minutes to relax. Literally stop thinking about what you're doing, what you did yesterday, or what you need to do next. You might go sit under a tree or take a walk in a quiet place or just close your eyes and breathe deeply. Try to focus on the breeze or the hum of a fan or a distant birdcall. Just these few things can have a big impact on your spiritual wellness.

At the end of the day, I believe that spirituality is in part a mental state that helps us to be better human beings.

Additionally, there's great spiritual healing in serving others. If we're paying attention, and our spiritual dimension is active, we can find all sorts of ways to make a difference in the lives of other people.

On Christmas Eve, we have a tradition to have a wonderful dinner as a family to celebrate and toast the New Year. We talk about the past year and the upcoming year and give each other gifts. It's a great time.

One year, however, because Karen was paying attention, we decided that instead of a big dinner on Christmas Eve we would go to a homeless shelter in Salt Lake City to help on the evening shift. When we arrived, the only workers there were the director and a few other helpers facing a very large group of homeless people—way too many for the shelter to manage. It was really sad. The big snow forecast for that night hadn't come yet, but it was pouring a cold, cold rain. Many of the people were soaked to the bone.

The director was thrilled that we were there and gave us a number of things to do. At one point we noticed a huge basket of umbrellas in the corner of the warehouse. Karen asked if it would it be okay to distribute the umbrellas, as many would be spending the night outside in the rain.

The director was hesitant, as the umbrellas needed to last the entire year, but he said we could give a few to some of the women. He said, "We really don't want to take you over to the men's section because it can get a little aggressive and hostile over there."

We started handing umbrellas to the women in the shelter, and they were so grateful. But they told us that the ones who truly needed them were the men outside in the pouring rain.

So we walked to the men's section accompanied by four armed security guards. They said, "Stay with us because we don't want anybody getting hurt." We were thinking, "What could happen? These people are homeless. They need some help." We walked outside with a handful of umbrellas, and the crowd started mobbing us to get one.

It was very scary. My son PJ saw somebody flashing a gun. Another had a knife. Some guys were on drugs or binged out on alcohol. Many had mental health issues. Some of them didn't even realize where they were because of the medications they were on.

But then PJ handed an umbrella to a guy who was only 18 or 19 years old. The young man had tears in his eyes when he looked at PJ and said, "This is the best gift I've ever been given." My son was so taken aback by that.

When we left later that evening, the director said, "We decided to give you guys all the umbrellas because the people were really responding to you. It was such a great thing for you to be able to do something meaningful for them. We wanted to say our thanks for your family coming at a time when we really needed some help."

We came away and shared our experiences for the rest of the evening. That was a whole different Christmas for us, to see and serve people who were truly in need.

Later that night, the rain turned into a foot and a half of snow. We realized we might have saved some lives with those umbrellas. The experience was a turning point for us.

We served for one evening in one shelter in one city. How many places are there in the world that is just like that homeless shelter, or worse? How many people are in need? It's almost overwhelming when you look at it that way, but even if you do one thing for one person in one place, you can make a difference.

Spiritual wellness is mental preparation for doing good, but you have to pay attention to see the good that is out there to be done. There are endless needs in every community in America.

APPLICATION

Baby Boomers and Spiritual Wellness

As Boomers move toward retirement, many of them will suffer from a loss of purpose. For many, it will be tough to lose the goals, the drive for the next level of achievement, the social connections with business friends. They will have trouble finding meaning in their days.[xxiv]

Still, Boomers have been called "the generation of seekers," the first generation to take their faith into their own hands instead of automatically adopting the faith of previous generations. I believe they will find greater meaning in serving others. Many will have the leisure to reach out and learn about the needs of people in their own communities—volunteering at schools, hospitals, homeless centers—wherever they are needed. Free of the need to go to work every day, they will find in serving individuals who really need help, the kind of spiritual satisfaction they're looking for.

Gen Xers and Spiritual Wellness

Gen Xers, for all their skepticism, are nevertheless more religious than Boomers. The security they lacked in childhood as latchkey kids they seem to find in faith groups such as nondenominational churches. This works for them to a degree, but given the kind of stress they live with, they need to find more opportunities for self-reflection and introspection.

The beta waves are strong with Gen Xers, to paraphrase Star Wars, and they suffer from a lack of time to invest in themselves and a more meaningful life. By adopting the suggestions in this chapter, they will find the inspiration and the spiritual rest they seek.

Millennials and Spiritual Wellness

Millennials are leaving organized religion behind to a great extent, but that doesn't mean they are any less spiritual than previous generations. They are also very invested in finding personal meaning.

They find spiritual uplift and healing in many non-traditional ways—by weightlifting or rock climbing, through meditation or yoga. They still gather for spiritual support: some spiritual gatherings are ad hoc, such as a "grief dinner" for a friend who has lost a loved one.

Urban Millennials in particular find meaning in community service: building affordable housing, workspaces, or shared gardens.

Because Millennials have grown up in a world of rich and abundant choices, they like to take their choice of spiritual devotions as well. Personally, though, I believe small acts of service for others are often the highest and best ways to create a meaningful life.

THE **WELLNESS 8**

Addendum

THE WELLNESS 8
ACROSS GENERATIONS

For tens of thousands of years, things just didn't change much from one generation to the next. Most people lived and died never having traveled more than a few miles from where they were born. Sons did what their fathers did, one generation after another; and daughters learned how to do the things their mothers did.

Things progressed very slowly until 1450 in Mainz, Germany, when Johannes Gutenberg had the profound insight to make a printing press with moveable type. Within a generation, information proliferated and the masses became literate. Social progress began—however slowly. By the mid 1700's, exploration, science, and technology started impacting lifestyle and brought people choices they'd never had before.

New worlds were open to exploration and new ideas were afloat. Don't like farming? Try your hand at business. No land available? There's plenty across the sea. Don't like that church? Try this one. For almost the first time in the history of mankind, people had options. Generations started to transition—to do things differently than their parents had done. But that transition has turned into an explosion of change in the last 75 years.

It's no surprise that anyone born since World War II (1945) sees things differently from the way their parents saw them. American thinker Buckminster Fuller proposed the "Knowledge Doubling Curve"—that until 1900 human knowledge (i.e., useful information) doubled approximately every century. By the end of World War II knowledge doubled every 25 years. Today, knowledge continues to escalate faster and faster. For example, nanotechnology knowledge is doubling every two years and medical knowledge every 18 months. Collective knowledge is doubling every 13 months. According to IBM, the building up of the "internet of things"—the vast connections among our phones, our cars, our homes, our workplaces—will lead to the doubling of knowledge every 12 hours.[xxv]

All of this new information has radically altered the world and the people who live in it. Options abound that previously did not exist. Old jobs regularly die and give birth to new occupations never before imagined. In 1900 farmers made up 31% of the work force. In 1950, that number had dropped to 12.2%.[xxvi] In 2000, farmers and those who work in agriculture made up less than one percent of the work force.[xxvii] Most of the occupations that kids who are currently in junior high school will do, have yet to be imagined.

In this book, we look at three different generations (or cohorts, as they are called by social scientists) and see how they relate to the W8:

- Baby Boomers (born between 1945 and 1965)

- Generation Xers (born between 1965 and 1979)

- Millennials (born between 1980 and 2000)

Although we shouldn't generalize too much, each group is unique in many ways. They have differing attitudes, opportunities, and challenges. At the end of each chapter, we'll talk about those differences and suggest some things to help you in your generation leverage the W8.

Let's look at the Baby Boomers first.

Baby Boomers

Baby Boomers were born between the mid-1940s and the mid-1960s. My parents were Baby Boomers, both born shortly after World War II when America's post-war productivity and general optimism was unequaled. Known as the Golden Age of Capitalism, it was a period of economic prosperity between 1945 and the early 1970s.

The Baby Boomers are the largest (76 million in America alone), the wealthiest, most active, and most physically fit generation that had ever lived, and probably the first ever to grow up genuinely expecting the world to improve with time.[xxviii] They had peak levels of income and reaped the benefits of abundant food, clothes, and education.

Boomers tend to think of themselves as a special generation, set apart and very different ("superior?") from those that came before. "Almost from the time they were conceived, Boomers were dissected, analyzed, and pitched to by modern marketers"[xxix] whose campaigns reinforced their sense of uniqueness and importance.

Don't believe me? Never before have there been commercials about E.D. and retirement options. The other night I watched the Beach Boys on TV. I think Mike Love, the only original member still singing, was in his early 70's. Dozens of aging bands tour for the Boomers, who come out in droves to see them—my mom has tickets for an upcoming Neil Diamond concert.

Boomers grew up at a time of dramatic social change. TV first made it's appearance in the age of the Boomers. Think of the hippie movement and the emerging drug culture in the late 1960s, and running a parallel track, the Vietnam War. Or Beatlemania and, later, Woodstock. There's hardly a Baby Boomer who can't tell you where they were when President Kennedy was shot, or when Neil Armstrong first stepped on the moon. Baby Boomers experienced:

- A time of unparalleled national optimism and prosperity

- The Cold War, fear of a nuclear attack from Russia, bomb shelters and hiding under their desk at school

- The assassination of President John F. Kennedy and later his brother Robert

- The assassination of Martin Luther King

- The confidence building from putting a man on the moon

- The incredible waste and destruction of the War in Vietnam

- The Civil Rights Movement

Boomers' Current Worries and Concerns

As a generation, Boomers have tended to avoid planning for death or any long-term planning at all, especially around finances. Some argue that Boomers remain in a state of denial about their own aging and death, and are leaving an undue economic burden on their Gen X and Millennial children for their retirement and care. According to a 2011 LifeGoesStrong.com survey[xxx] regarding Boomers, their main worries are economic:

- They can't pay their bills

- Most are unable to retire – 42% are delaying retirement and 25% claim they will never be able to retire. (They are still working, not because they want to, but they have to. How many Wal-Mart greeters can the US support?)

- As they age, their bodies are wearing out. They are concerned about health care.

- They desire a simpler, less expensive lifestyle, but don't know how to get it.

Generation X (aka, The Latchkey Generation)

Born between 1965 and 1979, Gen Xers bookended between the Baby Boomers (75 million strong) and the Millennials (80 million total), they were born at a time when society was focused less on children and more on adults. So they are known as "Generation X," the "latchkey generation," or even the "overlooked generation."

They were children during a time of shifting social values, with divorce rates doubling in the mid-1960s before peaking in 1980. Sometimes called the "latchkey generation," their parents both worked as they were growing up, so they lacked adult supervision—unlike the previous generation where the mother was mostly home and the father went out to a job.

As teens and young adults, they were dubbed the "MTV Generation" and characterized as slackers, as cynical and disaffected. But this isn't really the whole picture—not at all.

Current research describes Gen X adults as active, happy, and as achieving a work–life balance never attained by typical Boomers.[xxxii] The Gen X cohort has been credited with entrepreneurial tendencies. Social researchers describe Gen Xers as independent, resourceful, self-managing, adaptable, cynical, pragmatic, skeptical of authority, and as seeking a work life balance. [xxxiii xxxiv xxxv]

Harvard Business Review says Gen Xers "are already the greatest entrepreneurial generation in U.S. history; their high-tech savvy and marketplace resilience have helped America prosper in the era of globalization. [xxxvi]

According to authors Michael Hais and Morley Winograd, "Small businesses and the entrepreneurial spirit that Gen Xers embody have become one of the most popular institutions in America. There's been a recent shift in consumer behavior and Gen Xers will join the 'idealist generation' in encouraging the celebration of individual effort and business risk-taking. As a result, Xers will spark a renaissance of entrepreneurship in economic life, even as overall confidence in economic institutions declines. Customers, and their needs and wants (including those of Millennials) will become the North Star for an entire new generation of entrepreneurs". [xxxvii]

A 2015 study by Sage Group reports Gen Xers "dominate the playing field" with respect to founding startups in the United States and Canada, with Gen Xers launching the majority (55%) of all new businesses in 2015. [xxxviii]

Gen Xers were the first generation to experience:

- The highest level of education in the US to date

- The 1970s energy crisis and the first gas shortages in the US

- The fall of the Berlin Wall and the splitting apart of the Soviet Union

- MTV

- China's momentary flirtation with personal freedom and the tragedy of Tiananmen Square

- Fighting in the first Gulf War

- The disappearance of millions of American manufacturing jobs

Gen X Current Worries and Concerns

As the Boomers reluctantly get out of the way, Gen Xers are eager to take their place as business and government leaders. Gen Xers are becoming the majority in Congress and legislatures. Although they feel qualified and capable, with the Boomers' reluctance to retire, the big question is will the Boomers get out of the way fast enough?

Like the Boomers, Gen Xers are steadily marching on to retirement and, like Boomers, many don't have the money they need. Unlike Boomers, Gen Xers will struggle with the drain of national and personal resources caused by the Boomers. Gen Xers are concerned about:

- Taking care of the previous generation

- Draining of Social Security and health care funds

- Being effective parents

- Getting enough money for retirement

- Gaining more flexibility at work

Millennials

Millennials were born between 1980 and 2000. At 80 million strong, they are the biggest age cohort in American history. Primarily the children of Baby Boomers, they have come of age in an era when their parents tended to be extremely protective. Many grew up believing that they were all beautiful, perfect, and that they could have it all and be it all. According to social researcher Joel Stein, the word "entitlement" says it all. [xxxix]

Millennials interact with others all day, but almost entirely through screens. They love their phones but hate talking on them. They sit in coffee shops texting, often to people sitting right next to them. They might look calm, but they suffer from FOMO (Fear of Missing Out) a recognized social angst that others might be having rewarding experiences from which one is absent". This social anxiety is characterized by "a desire to stay continually connected with what others are doing". [xl] Seventy percent of them check their phones as many as three or four times an hour, looking for the dopamine hit they get from a new message. Half of them have all the symptoms of phone attachment addiction. Many also experience phantom pocket-vibration syndrome. [xli]

Many Millennials cannot comprehend living without the instant access to information that the omnipresent Internet provides. An editor of a tech magazine said he had no idea what it meant to be bored, as access to the world has always been in the palm of his hand.

Because they grew up believing in their innate superiority (but full of anxiety that they might get found out), this generation has the highest likelihood of having unmet expectations and the lowest levels of satisfaction with their jobs, one observer: "It is sort of a crisis of unmet expectations." [xlii]

On the other hand, as employees, Millennials are earnest and optimistic, driven by meaning and purpose, and by doing work that makes a difference. They tend to embrace the system and don't make waves. They are pragmatic idealists. They are pro-business. They have less household and credit-card debt than any previous generation on record—which might be the result of staying longer in their parents' homes.

They're not into going to church, even though they believe in God, because they don't identify with big institutions; one-third of adults under 30, the highest percentage ever, are religiously unaffiliated. [xliii]

Millennials were the first generation to:

- Have computers in the classrooms. And then on their desks. And then in their bedrooms. And then in their pockets.

- Take a photo without film.

- Use a digital camera.

- Use a cordless phone.

- Send a text message.

- Take a photo from a mobile phone.

- Grow up in a 24/7 news cycle.

- Watch a terrorist attack live on television, in the instance of 9/11.

- Grow up alongside social media - MySpace, Bebo, Facebook, Instagram, and Snapchat.

- Instantaneously share an image with millions of people.

- Create a video and upload it to YouTube.

Millennials' Current Worries and Concerns

The Miami Herald reports that Millennials are primarily worried about money—earning it and keeping it. But 41 percent admit to spending more on coffee last year than they invested in their retirement accounts. (Sounds like they're taking money management seriously!) Seventy percent feel their education did not prepare them to manage their finances, while just 5 percent of younger Millennials are actively investing. [xliv]

USA Today reports that Millennials also worry about finding a job or a career that aligns with their personal interests. Additional concerns of Millennials center on social and economic inequality and skepticism toward government, the media, and formal religion. Their top reason for selecting a job is to find meaning and make a positive difference in society. [xlv]

Generations and the Wellness 8

The generation you belong to has a lot of influence on how you use the Wellness 8, and that's okay. Millennials will have a different view of economic wellness than Boomers. Millennial ideas of career and retirement don't look much like Boomer ideas. Gen Xers tend to see their social lives as intimate and small while Boomers and Millennials are more likely to cast a wide net of friendships and relationships.

As you apply the Wellness 8, make sure to pause and consider how your generational outlook will affect your application of the W8. Don't assume you have to apply the W8 the way I do or the way others of different generations do.

You belong to a great generation, no matter what it is. Think about your own strengths, apply the principles of the W8 accordingly, and you'll have a great life, too.

REFERENCES AND NOTES

i.   The 7 Habits of Highly Effective Network Marketing Professionals, Audio CD, by Stephen R Covey, published by Franklincovey, April, 2009

ii.   http://www.childstudysystem.com/uploads/6/1/9/1/6191025/mindset_book_study.pdf

iii.   https://www.psychologytoday.com/blog/sapient-nature/201310/how-negative-is-your-mental-chatter, Raj Raghunathan, Ph.D.

iv.   http://www.businessinsider.com/jim-rohn-youre-the-average-of-the-five-people-you-spend-the-most-time-with-2012-7

v.   Man's Search for Meaning, by Viktor E Frankl, Beacon Press.

vi.   https://medlineplus.gov/ency/patientinstructions/000355.htm

vii.   https://www.forbes.com/sites/jordanshapiro/2015/11/03/teenagers-in-the-u-s-spend-about-nine-hours-a-day-in-front-of-a-screen/#42ed969aa7c9

viii.   http://www.nielsen.com/us/en/insights/reports/2015/the-total-audience-report-q4-2014.html

ix.   https://www.nytimes.com/2016/07/01/business/media/nielsen-survey-media-viewing.html

x.   http://www.slate.com/articles/technology/technology/2013/07/instagram_and_self_esteem_why_the_photo_sharing_network_is_even_more_depressing.html

xi.   The Worry Cure: Seven Steps to Stop Worry from Stopping You, by Robert L. Leahy, Ph.D. Potter/tenspeed/Harmony, 2005

xii.   Helen Rolfs, "Why Boomers Are Retiring to College," PBS newshour, Apr. 20, 2014.

xiii.   Silke Simonsi, "Next Generation Learning – How Millennials Shape L&D," swissvbs, Jul 15, 2016.

xiv.   https://www.bls.gov/news.release/pdf/nlsoy.pdf

xv.   https://business.linkedin.com/talent-solutions/resources/job-trends/job-seeker-trends-why-and-how-people-change-jobs-global?Trk=bl-po_new-research-reveals-the-real-reason-people-switch-jobs_Allison-Schnidman_080515

xvi.   https://www.nytimes.com/2014/06/01/opinion/sunday/why-you-hate-work.html?_r=1

xvii.   http://247wallst.com/special-report/2015/11/06/countries-spending-the-most-on-health-care-2/4/

xviii.   http://fortune.com/2016/09/22/america-healthiest-country/

xix.   https://news.byu.edu/news/stayin'-alive-that's-what-friends-are

xx.   http://journals.sagepub.com/doi/abs/10.1177/000312240607100301

xxi.   https://usatoday30.usatoday.com/news/nation/2006-06-22-friendship_x.htm The study is based on surveys of 1,531 people in 1985 and 1,467 in 2004, part of the General Social Survey by the National Opinion Research Center at the University of Chicago.

xxii.   *In Search of Stones*, M. Scott Peck, Hyperion; Reprint edition (May 9, 1996)

xxiii.   Lead the Field, Earl Nightingale, Simon & Schuster Audio/Nightingale-Conant; Abridged edition

xxiv.   https://www.usatoday.com/story/money/2015/02/03/baby-Boomers-retirement-emotional/22799155/

xxv.   http://www.industrytap.com/knowledge-doubling-every-12-months-soon-to-be-every-12-hours/3950

xxvi.   https://www.agclassroom.org/gan/timeline/farmers_land.htm

xxvii.   https://www.census.gov/prod/2003pubs/c2kbr-25.pdf. This surprisingly low percentage requires further explanation. Prior to the overhaul of the SOC, farm and ranch owners and renters were classified in the farming, fishing, and forestry occupations group. After the reclassification, they were put into the management, professional, and related occupations group.

xxviii.   Jones, Landon (1980), *Great Expectations: America and the Baby Boom Generation*, New York: Coward, mccann and Geoghegan

xxix.   Gillon, Steve (2004) *Boomer Nation: The Largest and Richest Generation Ever, and How It Changed America*, Free Press, "Introduction",

xxx.   *"Redefining Retirement: A Much Longer Lifespan Means More to Consider". Living Better at 50. Retrieved August 17, 2011.*

xxxi.   Howe, Neil (1992). *Generations: The History of America's Future, 1584 to 2069*

xxxii.   Howe, Neil (June 2007). "The next 20 years: How customer and workforce attitudes will evolve". Harvard Business Review. Retrieved 19 June 2016.

xxxiii. The metlife Study of Gen X: The MTV Generation Moves into Mid-Life" (PDF). Metlife. April 2013. Retrieved 19 June 2016.

xxxiv. *"CREATING A CULTURE OF INCLUSION -- LEVERAGING GENERA-TIONAL DIVERSITY: At-a-Glance" (PDF). University of Michigan. 2010. Retrieved 19 June 2016.*

xxxv. *White, Doug (23 December 2014). "What to Expect From Gen-X and Millennial Employees". Entrepreneur. Retrieved 19 June 2016.*

xxxvi. Howe, Neil "The next 20 years (see footnote viii)

xxxvii. http://www.beinkandescent.com/articles/942/genx

xxxviii. https://www.sage.com/na/~/media/site/sagena/responsive/docs/startup/report

xxxix. Millennials: The Me Me Me Generation, Joel Stein, Time Magazine, May 20, 2013, http://time.com/247/millennials-the-me-me-me-generation/

xl. Anderson, Hephzibah (16 April 2011). "Never heard of Fomo? You're so missing out". *The Guardian.*

xli. Ibid., Joel Stein, "Millennials" (see footnote xv)

xlii. *Managing the New Workforce: International Perspectives on the Millennial Generation,* by Eddy S. Ng, Sean Lyons, Linda Schweitzer, Edward Elgar Publishing, 2014

xliii. Ibid., Joel Stein, "Millennials" (see footnote xv)

xliv. http://www.miamiherald.com/news/business/article126068924.html#storylink=cpy

xlv. https://www.usatoday.com/story/money/2015/10/25/survey-Millennials-around-world-worry-most-economic-inequality/74583976/

About The Author

Jeremy Reynolds, husband and father, entrepreneur and personal development guru is the founder and CEO of Well-Beyond, a nutritional direct selling and personal growth company.

Named Master Distributor of direct selling company, Xocai in 2005, Jeremy teaches people how to live more fulfilling lives and how to generate life-changing income. Jeremy has traveled to 40+ countries around the world, sharing personal growth and financial success principles with over a half a million people worldwide.

About Wellness 8

To learn more about the eight dimensions of wellness please visit our website at www.TheWellness8.com.

About directSMARTS Publishing

directSMARTS

directSMARTS is a content publisher and online training platform for network marketers who want to learn the necessary skills to grow their businesses. On the platform, successful direct sellers share their skills, knowledge, personal development principles, and experience with others who are eager to learn. Learn more at directSMARTS.com.

A FREE Gift From The Breethe App

Go to www.thewellness8.com/breethe for your FREE Balance Breath audio download and a discount promo code for complete Breethe app access.

This app is available for both the Apple and Android operating systems.

Description

The easiest way to meditate! De-stress & sleep better in only 10 min with your personal meditation coach! Learn simple mindfulness and meditation techniques to help you bring more happiness, calm and peace of mind into your life.

Relax, reduce your stress, sleep better, sharpen your mind, and improve your relationships – in just 10 minutes a day!

This meditation app includes hundreds of daily meditations, and a wide variety of other guided meditations to help you deal with specific issues such as weight loss, insomnia, anxiety, work performance, trouble sleeping, etc. It even has a mindfulness program for kids.

Selected Best New App by Apple in 95 countries.

About The 7 Habits of Highly Effective Network Marketing Professionals

Audio CD and workbook

By Stephen R. Covey

In this 2-CD training, Stephen R. Covey presents an integrated, principle-centered approach for becoming a highly effective network marketing professional. Including real-world examples of current, successful networkers, Covey reveals a step-by-step pathway for not only living with fairness, integrity, service, and human dignity, but applying principle-centered habits that will help you become truly effective in your networking business.

Included in this training is a 48-page workbook outlining timeless networking principles that, along with the audio training, acts as the perfect complement to help you achieve your ultimate networking goals of effectiveness.

Disc 1: Approximately 48 minutes

Disc 2: Approximately 44 minutes

Available on the FranklinCovey website at:

http://store.franklincovey.com/the-7-habits-of-highly-effective-network-marketing-professionals-audio-cd

Made in the USA
San Bernardino, CA
07 October 2017